Art Textiles of the World

Great Britain Volume 2

Edited by Jennifer Harris

Sally Freshwater
Hush

Contents

Michael Brennand-Wood
Twelve Dreams Within The Here And Now

Introduction

Alice Kettle
Man and Tree II

Contemporary textiles practice is a very broad church. It encompasses fashion, design, fine art, craft and architecture. Because of this breadth and in order to achieve some visual and conceptual coherence for this survey the artists whose work is featured represent an area of textiles practice more closely allied to painting and sculpture than to design. Some, indeed, began their careers as painters and sculptors but found in cloth, stitch, dyeing or printing the best medium in which to express their artistic vision.

Like a painter Jo Budd exploits the tonal variations in her dyed and printed fabrics to convey shifting impressions of light at different seasons and at different times of day. The play of light on cloth is more seductive than on oil or gouache. She 'mixes' colour by layering different sheer fabrics, and puts in stitches to create different tensions in the cloth. The sewing machine allows Alice Kettle to 'draw' with stitches and to apply broad, painterly sweeps of colour in silk, cotton and metallic threads. She 'overpaints' by repeatedly stitching over some areas of the cloth, which creates fluid, rippling three-dimensional surfaces and shadows. Janet Ledsham dyes and layers the fleece from sheep in a painterly manner, but the result is soft and multi-dimensional. It is this tactile, third dimension which is unavailable to the painter and which allows an appeal to the viewer's sense of touch as well as sight. Michael Brennand-Wood has said that "once you start to use textiles it is difficult to go back, you become sensitised to the tactility." [1]

Textiles are particularly suited to three-dimensional sculptural forms, and sculpture, more than the other fine arts, draws on crafts sensibilities. Sculpture has changed more dramatically in the twentieth century than at any other time in history. It has seen its techniques, its materials and its concerns all repeatedly challenged, and sculptors today use every conceivable material to make art. In her 1979 essay 'Sculpture in the Expanded Field', the American art historian Rosalind Krauss, looking back at a decade of developments within sculpture, wrote how

"Over the last ten years rather surprising things have come to be called sculpture: narrow corridors with TV monitors at the ends, large photographs documenting country hikes, mirrors placed at strange angles in ordinary rooms, temporary lines cut into the floor of the desert".

demonstrating how a cultural term can be expanded until it is in danger of collapsing in on itself. [2] This same questioning of categories has been happening within contemporary textiles practice during the 1980s and '90s.

In this volume the work of Janet Ledsham, Shelly Goldsmith, Sally Freshwater, Caroline Broadhead and Rushton Aust all exploits the sculptural possibilities of textiles. Sally Freshwater's work, with its references to sails, kites, awnings and parasols, has been developed from a preoccupation with space, volume and the tensile properties of fabric. In Shelly Goldsmith's more recent work traditional Gobelin tapestry is a three-dimensional construction, not constrained by the gallery walls, representing a departure from the contemporary interest in flat woven wall hangings. In her *Sallagh* series, Janet Ledsham has taken fine lengths of felt into the landscape, where the natural vegetation becomes confused with the leaf patterns embedded in the felt fibres. These interventions exist only in the form of high resolution photographs which aim to record the transient effects of the play of light and have elicited comparisons with the work of sculptors such as Andy Goldsworthy. Finally, in Caroline Broadhead's *The Waiting Game* (cover photograph), the sculptural possibilities of textiles expand into installation and theatre.

Cloth is a medium with powerful associations for most of us because of the centrality of fabric in human culture. Textiles are ubiquitous and each of us has a personal relationship with them. We clothe ourselves and adorn our environment with them, and they reveal as well as conceal our identities, our ideological values and our aspirations. Cloth has the capacity to carry richly layered social and cultural conventions. It has always possessed semiotic potential as well as being a vehicle for the fruits of human labour and virtuoso artistry. Tapestry weaver Lesley Millar has commented that, unlike other materials associated with the making of art – bronze, oil, paint or stone, for example – we all have an understanding of and can bring our own distinct reading to cloth when it is used to create a work of art.[3] Several of the artists profiled in this volume refer to the universality of cloth, our instinctive understanding of it, as one of the qualities which drew them to use it in their work in preference to other materials.

Textiles have their own aesthetic concerns and a long, rich history on which to draw, although this history has sometimes failed to receive due recognition because of textiles' close association with domesticity and with the history of women.[4] Janet Ledsham draws on the craft traditions of the rural Irish culture which inspires her work, particularly the patchwork quilts which the women made. Lesley Mitchison's work is also rich in historical reference. The garments which she makes are metaphors for constraint and memory; they have a real, practical history and a symbolic potency. And possibly more than any of the other artists Michael Brennand-Wood's work over the last twenty years has aimed at a conceptual synthesis of contemporary and historical sources. Even where no textiles are used in the making of the work it specifically addresses the status of textiles within contemporary visual arts practice.

As an art practice textiles are currently enjoying a period of consolidation and development in Great Britain. A wave of recent major exhibitions [5] has fuelled the debate around the 'space' in which the practice operates and suggests that art textiles are coming of age. Clothing and textiles have had a significant effect on twentieth-century artistic practice.[6] Since the 1960s Eva Hesse, Miriam Schapiro, Rosemarie Trockel and others have all used cloth as a transgressive medium, for its capacity to challenge hierarchies and question assumptions. Sculptors such as Claes Oldenburg have challenged the primacy of monumental materials and commemorative subjects by re-creating hard, everyday objects – telephones, typewriters, drainpipes – in soft materials, including cloth. As an expressive medium textiles are free of the weight and traditions

Janet Ledsham
Mustard Hill (detail)

associated with formalist art history. Textiles can challenge the hegemony of painting and sculpture, where "histories and values are already written, meanings are already given, and spaces . . . already delineated for [their] reception." [7]

During the last thirty years textile art has emerged as a distinct critical practice which operates in a borderland between fine art and craft. In the catalogue to a recent exhibition at the Serpentine Gallery in London of work by fine artists who use cloth and thread as metaphor, Lisa Corrin, the exhibition curator, describes thread as "a material that cuts across cultures, classes, gender and historical time," arguing that its ability to migrate across boundaries (of medium and genre) makes it an "ideal expression of an aesthetic of displacement within contemporary art." [8]

In a similar vein, Sarat Maharaj has talked of an 'edginess' to avantgarde textiles practice which destabilises the boundaries between genres.[9] In his personal statement in this volume Rushton Aust identifies a fascination with edges, and an affinity with those communities, cultures and individuals which operate at the margins. Polly Binns also sees her work as lying on an edge, a shifting boundary informed by both fine art and craft practices, like the intertidal zone of the North Norfolk coastline that has inspired all of her work in the past decade. And Caroline Broadhead's work, in particular, has always been about dissolving boundaries – between jewellery and garment, clothing and self, body and psyche, outside and inside.

Clothing has held a particular fascination for artists in the twentieth century. In the 1920s Vera Stepanova, Alexander Rodchenko, Lyubov Popova and others in the Soviet Union turned to fashion as a rebellion against traditional easel art:

> "under pressure from the revolutionary conditions of contemporaneousness we reject the pure forms of art. We recognise self-sufficient easel art as being useless. We declare productivist art to be absolute and contruction to be its only form of expression." [10]

Polly Binns
Sand Sections No. 8

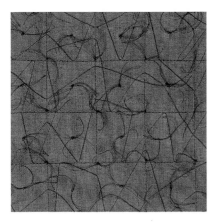

Since the 1960s significant numbers of artists have made art through the vehicle of clothes precisely because everyone is literate in cloth and it is thus an artistic medium accessible to all. Dress is central to the way we view ourselves and project our personalities and taste. From Christo's landmark *Wedding Dress* of 1967 – a package of some 100 sq metres of white satin pulled by a young woman with silk ropes which served as a metaphor for the burden of middle-class marriage – numerous artists have gone on to make non-functional, metaphorical clothing to explore issues around the body and identity. Nick Vaughn, Marian Schoettle and Beverly Semmes have all, like Caroline Broadhead, made clothes whose exaggerated or multiple elements startle and unnerve, and clothing continues to exert a fascination for a younger generation of artists – Louise Richardson, Emily Bates and Stephen Willats all subvert in some way the familiarity of everyday garments to challenge or unsettle us. Indeed, so many artists have made art involving clothing that it has been the subject of a number of major exhibitions. *Conceptual Clothing*, initiated by the Ikon Gallery in Birmingham in 1986, was one of the first; several have been organised by US galleries in the '90s. [11]

Having made jewellery which interacted with the body Caroline Broadhead began to make garments in the early 1980s. These acted as a metaphor for the body and articulated ideas about the self and identity, in particular a feminine identity. From 1996 the shadows of garments began to assume an integral, and sometimes more important, role in her installations. Her intention was "to give emphasis to the hidden, non-existent and immaterial . . . to give it 'body' or form."[12]

Lesley Mitchison
Making Clothes for Children I

Clothes hold the visual memory of a person, they are heavy with emotional presence , which is one of the reasons why they are so potent as metaphors. The imprint of personal identity, in addition to the symbolic potency of garments with such obvious references to constraint, promiscuity and suppression, initially drew Lesley Mitchison to the study of the historical corsets and other foundation garments on which she based her metaphorical undergarments of the early 1990s. Finely woven, printed and embroidered cloths were deliberately 'distressed' by cutting and burning in order to capture the sense of wear and tear apparent in the originals. Her most recent work, inspired by a collection of paper garments at the War Memorial Museum in Canberra, is even more directly about memory invested in clothing and the vulnerability of textile fibres to wear and the ravages of time.

Textile art has tended to suffer from the (historically recent) belief that real art is the result of creative thought rather than a result of the process of making. In defining work as textile art one is emphasizing the importance of materials and process. For the textile artist, however, the process of making is a conscious, investigative act and all the artists featured here combine consummate craft skills with a strong sense of the conceptual possibilities of materials and form.

In a recent interview with Pamela Johnson, Caroline Broadhead compared the process of making to forensic science; she sees herself as making work in order to discover feelings or an inner state. [13] Her work has possibly less material presence than that of any of the other artists, and yet this engagement with materials is still present in what Johnson describes as her "barely made" new work. In *Still Light*, for example, she carried out experiments with a variety of threads before settling on the fine, transparent elastic used in the final installation. Jo Budd also claims that the process of exploration involved in making allows her to discover what it is that interests her as an artist.

Polly Binns's methodology has similarly been described as close to "the process of enquiry a researcher in the sciences might undertake." [14] She repeatedly walks the same landscape – a stretch of saltmarshes and tidal inlets, which alters with each tide and season – tracing, exploring and committing it to memory. Although photographs form a part of her accumulated memory the resulting work is not created from these nor from sketches. It is, rather, a non-literal evocation of the patterns which she finds in nature, the result of an interplay between perception and memory. As with Jo Budd, the work is not a topographical recording of an actual scene, but more an illusion of the artist's experience of landscape. And even though work may be visualised during this process of walking it continues to evolve in the studio "as it offers its own qualities back."

Textiles has its own language, derived from an understanding of the materials and processes involved and from its history, techniques and traditions. For Sally Freshwater, exploiting the tensile qualities of fabric structures requires practical knowledge of how a surface feels and will behave. Process for her is more of a struggle, an actual physical fight between the fabric and the structure of her pieces, between the pliable and the solid elements. Tapestry is also a physically demanding medium which requires an enormous investment of time and deliberation, of weaving, unweaving and re-weaving. Shelly Goldsmith describes weaving as a decision-making process, during which issues are explored, and claims a fundamental relationship in her work between skill and content.

Much of the work described and illustrated in this volume defies easy categorisation. To define it as textile art valorizes the expressiveness of cloth and its history and suggests a debt to craft skills as well as an emphasis on content associated with fine art. However, Pennina Barnett has written that using terms such as 'textile art' and 'fibre art' seems to infer that there is still something to prove, although she concedes that, for the present, they are probably the best we have for describing non-functional work in textiles. [15]

Other writers on textiles are beginning to disagree, arguing that perhaps the distinctiveness of textile art as an umbrella label may be outliving its usefulness as borders become more elastic. [16] Fine artists have discovered that textiles are a particularly effective medium for exploring, for example, ideas around gender, the body, identity and domesticity. As categories and labels blur even further we may find that work in textiles grouped together because they share a common medium have less to do with each other than they have with sculpture, painting or mixed media works exploring similar issues.

It was illuminating to see Caroline Broadhead's work displayed alongside work by fine artists which has used clothing as a visual language at the Hayward Gallery in London in the exhibition *Addressing the Century: 100 Years of Art and Fashion* (1998-9). And in *Textures of Memory* at Angel Row Gallery in Nottingham (1999), curated by Pennina Barnett and Pamela Johnson, an exhibition exploring the personal relationships which we all have with cloth and the memories which it carries, textile artists are showing with artists working in video, photography, painting and sculpture. Similarly, it would be interesting to see Michael Brennand-Wood exhibit with others who share his interest in the potency and cultural significance of pattern-making – Chris Ofili, for example.

And yet, unlike the many fine artists who have appropriated textiles for its symbolic qualities the artists featured here do share a sense that the materials, techniques or history of textiles are somehow integral to their work and its conceptual basis, even though the work has implications far beyond the consideration of medium.

Shelly Goldsmith
Bathymetric – The Longest River IV

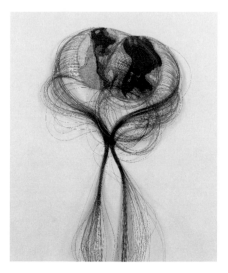

The breaking down of boundaries between different types of artistic practice is both exciting and deeply challenging to an art establishment such as that in Great Britain which is still dominated by the constraints of fine and applied art or art and craft. For what the debate about categories and definitions of 'space' for non-functional art textiles highlights is the fact that the disciplines themselves are too narrowly defined. Textile art does not need to define itself in relation to fine art for there is no distinction between the two at the level of ambition and achievement attained by the artists profiled in this volume. For some the medium is the message, but what matters to all is that their work communicates challenging ideas and arouses powerful emotions.

Dr Jennifer Harris

Deputy Director and Curator of Textiles, The Whitworth Art Gallery, Manchester

NOTES

1. Pamela Johnson, *Michael Brennand-Wood, You Are Here* (Hare Print Press, Sandy, Bedfordshire, 1999), p.11.
2. Rosalind Krauss, 'Sculpture in the Expanded Field', in Hal Foster (ed.), *Postmodern Culture* (Pluto Press, 1985), I am grateful to Pennina Barnett for bringing this article to my notice. She made the connection with textiles in an unpublished conference paper given at the Whitworth Art Gallery in May 1997.
3. Lesley Millar, 'An Introduction to Revelation', in *Revelation* (National Museum of Modern Art, Kyoto, 1998), p.88.
4. Conversely, feminist art historians have recovered and re-valued traditional 'feminine' and domestic crafts.
5. For example, *Under Construction* (Crafts Council Gallery, London, 1996), *The Woven Image* (Barbican Centre, London, 1996), *Art Textiles* (Bury St. Edmunds Art Gallery, 1996-8), *Flexible 1* (Oberfrankenhalle, Bayreuth, 1994), *Flexible 2 and Flexible 3* (Textielmuseum, Tilburg, 1997 and 1999).
6. Mildred Constantine and Laurel Reuter, *Whole Cloth* (Monacelli Press, New York, 1997) demonstrates that there has been traffic between art and textiles in all directions throughout the twentieth century.
7. Eilean Hooper-Greenhill in *Take 4: new perspectives on the British art quilt* (Telos Art Publishing and The Whitworth Art Gallery, 1998), p.45.
8. Lisa Corrin, 'Hanging by a Thread', in *Loose Threads* (Serpentine Gallery, London, 1998), p.41.
9. Sarat Maharaj, 'Arachne's Genre: Towards Intercultural Studies in Textiles', in *Journal of Design History*, vol. 4, no. 2, 1991, p.93.
10. Constantine and Reuter, *op.cit.*, p.192.
11. Constantine and Reuter, p.203 enumerates these.
12. Caroline Broadhead, 'Me and My Shadow', in *Crafts*, no. 157, March/April 1999, p.42.
13. *Bodyscape: Caroline Broadhead* (Angel Row Gallery, Nottingham and Northern Gallery for Contemporary Art, Sunderland, 1999), p.23.
14. Andrew Patrizio, 'A Vast Stereophony : Art and Research on Location', in *Location: Polly Binns and Shirley Chubb* (Kings Lynn Arts Centre, 1998), p.9.
15. Pennina Barnett, Foreword, *Revelation, op.cit.*, p.83.
16. See, for example, Judith Duffey, 'Textile Thinking: Continuity and Craft', in *Art Textiles* (Bury St. Edmunds Art Gallery, 1996) and Catherine Amidon, 'Is there still a place for fiber art?', in *FIBERARTS*, Nov/Dec 1997 pp.42.

Jo Budd

Fire and Ice –
Elemental Landscape Series

Janet Ledsham

The cycles of nature, of growth, decay and regeneration are inherent to the countryside. These processes find a resonance in the way I approach my work as well as in the images which it reflects.

Sallagh IV (1993)
photography, felt, plant materials
60 x 81cm

A first visit to Ireland was a matter of chance and it came as something of a delight and surprise. Then in 1972 I moved permanently to live in Northern Ireland. My home is in an unspoiled rural environment on the coast of County Antrim, which faces eastward to Scotland across the Irish Sea. Immediately to the west hangs the basalt cliffs of Sallagh Braes, one of the many escarpments and glens which give the coastal Antrim plateau its scenic character. The surrounding area is still littered with the artefacts, graves and raths of a prehistorical neolithic culture which farmed the slopes of the plateau and robbed it of its ancient woodland. Needless to say, this landscape which surrounds me, with its rich blend of topography, history and rural Irish culture, has provided me with recurring themes and sources of inspiration for my imagery.

I have made successive pilgrimages to the moorland plateau of County Antrim and the Derryveagh mountains in County Donegal. My particular fascination with both these places have been the peat cuttings or 'Turbary', as they are known locally. The blanket bog becomes scarred with the peat cuttings, which follow the contours of the landscape for miles. The rhythmic activity of cutting the turf with the spade makes repetitive rectangular patterns, and it is these patterns that have found their way into my work. So too have the textural surfaces of the old bog face, where organic debris has been revealed and where the regenerative process of colonizing mosses and lichens has begun.

In the early '80s I sketched on location with needle and thread. These were small, modest pieces of work which served as an initial source of reference. At the same time I made photographic records, building up a resource of images and places which has enabled me to integrate and synthesize elements from different sources and locations. This is particularly helpful when I am planning larger and more complicated compositions which may have a formal structure. Fifteen years ago I started constructing felted surfaces using the natural fleece from sheep. I trained initially as a painter so that it was no coincidence that I began to use the fleece in a painterly manner, dyeing it and overlapping the fibres to suggest the natural layering which is to be found in field textures as they change through the seasons. My aim has always been to develop the properties of the materials rather than to gain control over the outcome of the technique. Feltmaking is akin to alchemy and I began to develop a process which involves incorporating natural plant material into the felt. There is tremendous variability in the sizes and shapes of the plant material, ranging from minute seed heads of grasses and flowers such as primroses to larger elements of the structures of deciduous leaves of broad-leafed trees.

The fundamental and inevitable cycles of nature, the presence of growth, decay and regeneration are inherent to the countryside. Through continual experiment and innovation I would like to think that these elemental processes of nature find a resonance and a metaphor in the way I approach my work, as well as in the images which it reflects. I collect decomposing leaves in winter from the matted, dense undergrowth. I particularly look for the skeletonized leaves of poplar, maple and magnolia which, when excavated from the litter, appear ghost-like and ethereal. When they are incorporated into the composition of the work they seem to be both literally and figuratively caught in a time-warp of thin translucent and transparent fibres.

My aim has always been to develop the properties of the materials rather than to gain control over the outcome of the technique. Feltmaking is akin to alchemy and I began to develop a process which involves incorporating natural plant material into the felt. There is tremendous variability in the sizes and shapes of the plant material, ranging from minute seed heads of grasses and flowers such as primroses to larger elements of the structures of deciduous leaves of broad-leafed trees. *Sunshine and Shadows* (right and overleaf) refers to a particular geometric pattern used in traditional patchwork construction.

Sunshine and Shadows (1989) (detail)
felt, plant material, text
137 x 137cm

Recent explorations involve intertwining large branches of ash and elder with delicate and transparent lengths of felt. The visual and textural contrasts between these elements is extreme; by combining them and making full use of the compressions and tensions inherent in the construction I can, in sculptural terms, evoke echoes of the woodland canopy.

In addition to using the landscape as a source I have also looked at the craft traditions of the people who have always lived on this land. Most families today still own a patchwork quilt probably made by a member of the family from an earlier generation. It is interesting to observe the contrasting values which are placed upon this household item. The quilt may have become a cherished family heirloom or it could have found a more utilitarian function as an improvised covering for a haystack. The quilt has been an important source of inspiration for me in terms of the colours used but, perhaps more importantly, in terms of the formal geometric patterns on which the principles of patchwork are based, and I try to achieve in my work a personal translation of these. I am particularly interested in the motif known as 'ninepatch' and I use this configuration to give structural coherence to my work, to balance and constrain the potentially chaotic amalgam of organic materials. In retrospect, it seems that I have always employed this formal counterpoint of geometry and chaos.

My research into the Irish quilt has revealed that since the nineteenth century quiltmakers have used personal letters as paper templates to save them the expense of procuring other materials. I have adapted this idea, reversing the original arrangement of material and template to bring the paper and raw edges to the front of the work. The addition of selected texts to the work also provides strategic clues as to the identity of the maker, and thus to an intimate state of mind.

Many of the traditions, customs and even ways of dressing which prevailed in Ireland until the beginning of this century can be seen to be reflected in the ethnic cultures of many other countries. Similarly, work such as *Canopy* has been influenced by both the eighteenth-century capes found preserved in the bogs of Ireland and also by the *kepenek*, which is made and worn by shepherds in parts of Central Asia and Mongolia. Further layers of reference also infiltrate the 'Cape' series, particularly memories of my early life within the family, of the joys and tribulations of growing up, and of marrying and coping with the deaths of grandparents and parents. The work which I am involved with at present brings together all these preoccupations, while the intimate texts which I used earlier in the patchwork-related work have also found their way again into my most recent mixed media installations.

The quality of light in Ireland is exceptionally beautiful. The Atlantic winds sweep inland across the interior from the west and north coasts with such force as to create endless changing patterns of light and dark as the clouds move swiftly over the whole surface of the country. The purple-bronze tones of the heathers, the golden-yellow flowers of the gorse or 'whin' bushes, and the speckled whites of the bog cotton create a dazzling display of colours in the sunshine, only to be diffused or wiped out in seconds by the effects of this all-powerful weather. I deliberately tried to represent this phenomenon in *Sunshine and Shadows*, the title of which refers to a particular geometric pattern used in patchwork construction.

Sunshine and Shadows (1989)
felt, plant material, text
137 x 137cm

My photographic works, which are a further strategy and extension of my textile work, try to capture the elusive sense of light and luminosity. I take exceptionally fine lengths of felt outdoors and site them in natural vegetation to provide a foreground layer of imagery. The leaf patterns embedded in the felt fibres combine with distorted shadows of leaves and branches behind the felt. My aim here is to record the transient play of light as it illuminates the images which fleetingly occur.

In the photographs I try to capture a moment in time which magically suggests a particular mood, nuances of light and atmosphere, and a sense of both place and occasion. It is fair to say that these are qualities which all my work (on every scale from transient experiments to formal installations) strives to express. In many ways, it has always been that the spiritual and the functional find their expression within the one artefact.

Many of the traditions, customs and even ways of dressing which prevailed in Ireland until the beginning of this century can be seen reflected in the ethnic cultures of many other countries. Similarly, work such as *Canopy* (left) has been influenced both by the eighteenth-century capes found preserved in the bogs of Ireland and also by the *kepenek* which is made and worn by shepherds in areas of Central Asia and Mongolia.

Canopy (1992)
handmade felt,
plant material, machine stitch
147 x 123cm

right:
Veils of Courtship (1999) (detail)
text, handmade felt and paper, plant material, wire, fruit
canes
300 x 150 x 140cm

Born   1944, Wigan, Lancashire

Education

1963-66   Dip AD (Hons) Fine Art, Manchester Polytechnic
1966-67   Postgraduate Textiles, Manchester Polytechnic

Exhibitions: Solo

1999   Ormeau Baths Gallery, Belfast
1999   *Retrospective*, Drumcroon Art Centre, Wigan, Lancashire
1995   *Felts/Photographs,* The Gallery in the Forest, Grizedale, Cumbria

Exhibitions: Group

1998-9   *Connections, California Fibers and Celtic Felters*, Atheneum, La Jolla, California (tour)
1997-9   *European Art Quilts,* touring to Nederlands Textielmuseum, Tilburg, Holland and Denmark
1998   *50/50, The Challenge of Constraint,* 62 Group show, Tel Aviv, Israel (tour)
1997   *The Jerwood Prize for Applied Arts: Textiles,* short-list exhibition, Crafts Council Gallery, London
1996   Three-person exhibition *Contemporary British Textile Art,* Hordaland, Kunstnersentrum, Bergen, Norway
1996   *Art Textiles 96,* Bury St Edmunds Art Gallery (tour)
1996   *Regards sur le Feutre,* Musée du Chapeau, Chazelles-sur-Lyon, France
1996   *Whites Transparencies – Light,* 1ère du Lin en Haute Normandie, Abbée de Notre Dame du Bec, Paris
1994   *A Renaissance of Irish Craft,* Philadelphia Arts Association, USA
1994   *Felt Directions*, Collins Gallery, Glasgow and tour of France
1993-4   *Flexible 1,* Oberfrankenhalle, Bayreuth, Germany (tour: Holland, Poland, England)
1993   *Textiel + Europa* (tour: England, Belgium, Denmark, Germany, Holland)
1992-3   *62 Group*, Foyer Gallery, University of Ulster, Belfast (tour: Glasgow, London, Japan)
1992   *Feutres*, Musée du Feutre, Mouzon, France
1990-1   *Ulster Needlework, A Continuing Tradition,* Texas, USA
1990   *17 from the 62 Group,* Hankyu Department Store, Japan
1990   *International Felt Exhibition*, Den Gamle By, Denmark
1989   *Feutre Contemporain, Reliefs et Sculpture,* Musée du Feutre, Mouzon, France
1986   *Exposition International de Miniatures Textiles Contemporains,* Luxembourg
1985   *Neuf artistes des Mini Textiles de Strasbourg,* La Filotèque DMC, Paris
1984-5   *Contemporary British Textile Art,* 62 Group, Kokusai Galleries, Japan (tour)
1984   *Fifth International Biennial of Miniature Textiles*, Hungary (tour of Europe)

Professional

1998-   Reader in Textile Art, University of Ulster, Belfast
1976-97   Lecturer, University of Ulster, Belfast, Faculty of Art andf Design

Over the last twenty years the defining characteristic of my work has been a sustained commitment to the conceptual synthesis of contemporary and historical sources, in particular the exploration of three-dimensional line, structure and pattern. I believe that the most innovative textiles emanate from an assured understanding of both textile technique and history.

The majority of my earlier work focused upon an investigation of stitch structures and instinctive negative reaction to the excesses of surface decoration often associated with embroidered fabrics. I became interested in paring down the stitch, removing as much of the ground as was physically possible, to render the linear geometrical purity of the stitch structure. I perceived a direct parallel between the act of drawing in two dimensions and stitching three-dimensionally in space; both were essentially mark-making systems. As the work developed my initial interest in thread structures expanded into the assemblage and layering of surfaces within which a disparate collection of materials was laminated together. I enjoyed the spontaneous interaction and tension that could result from off-setting one surface against another, especially those not normally considered together.

Materials, I came to realise, had a spirit. Artists should be responsive to the inherent qualities of a given material and use it accordingly. Whether the approach be purist or iconoclastic, the end result should be in harmony with all the senses. The materials I select emanate from different sources; some are purchased new, the majority collected and stored over a long period of time. Historically, I have used almost everything: paper, wood, metal, stone, objects, glass, books, thread and textiles, perhaps one of the most emotive of all materials. Textiles have a touch, feel, smell, weight and colour. They are rich in social, political, cultural and historical associations.

The grid, which formed the basis of my work until the early 1980s, offered an ordered yet flexible ground. The wooden grid was in effect an exploded enlarged warp and weft structure. *El-Rayo X* (1981) formed part of a series that explored depth and translucency in relation to stitched structures. The primary influences in this work are microscopy and music, specifically the minimal pieces of Philip Glass, Terry Riley and Steve Reich. In 1980 I heard *Einstein on the Beach* by Philip Glass, a five-hour opera without conventional plot, arias or scenes. Short spoken texts are set against repetitive electronic keyboard rhythms played at frenetic speed. *El-Rayo X* was an attempt to reflect an aspect of that experience. Additive and subtractive layers of colour, paper and fabric are built up, obscured and revealed to expose at random a sense of their original meaning. The rhythmic base is overlaid by a metronomic stitched pulse of thread that runs throughout the whole work. The construction allows the viewer to jump between an awareness of detail and whole, between order and chaos.

Whilst acknowledging that my primary response to textiles had been an investigation of media and process, by the mid-1980s I had become increasingly interested in textile history, specifically carpets and stitched *suzani* cloths as a source for contemporary ideas. I wanted to make work that recognised the strength and integrity of early patterned textiles, acknowledging their use of loose geometry and sequential elements. I also wanted to question the derisory manner in which textiles continue to be discussed within the wider spectrum of the visual arts. Patterning and decoration in particular were used as critical terms to indicate either a lack of ideas or superfluous overworking.

My work has a strong physical presence. *Overlays* is over 30cm deep and weighs 150 kilos. Instinctively I have always been interested in the relationship between traditional textile materials and alternative media.

previous page:
You are Here (1997)
inlaid fabric. electric lights,
painted wood base
175 x 350 x 4cm

Overlays (1991)
books, paper, wood, ceramic, fabric,
thread, metal, cane, acrylic and relief
170 x 170 x 30cm

Historically, lace is a non-gender specific fabric, which was worn by both men and women, largely to indicate wealth, status and culture. Many of the early designs were of great complexity and influenced interior design and architectural detail. Today lace is primarily associated with lingerie fabric, its rich sense of history lost. I wished to reclaim lace for both men and women, forcing a re-evaluation of the potency and sophistication of early lace designs.

Slow Turning (1989) was directly influenced by the study of carpet designs, specifically the Buddhist 'cloud collar', a circular mantra that allowed the soul access to another world. The relief contains substantial textile references; fragments of Indian patched fabrics, Victorian upholstery and Indonesian ikat patternings transposed on to metal, wood and cloth. The central circle can be spun by hand, to create new optical and historical, cultural alignments of data. As the circle moves percussive sounds are generated to encourage additional movement.

above:
Underwater Moonlight (1997)
inlaid fabric into painted wood base
120 x 220 x 4cm

Overlays (1991) references the Lucy Lippard book of the same name. Topographical and ethnographic sources are interrelated to evoke a passage through time and space. The examination of materials within the work, both conceptual and physical, is an important aspect. Layered shapes and patterns act as mnemonic devices, triggering memories of place, experience and altered realities.

In 1992 I began a radical new series of work inspired by lace and interlaced fabrics, emanating from my research into historical textiles. Lace, long regarded as the most archetypal of feminine fabrics, with its questionable allusions to fragility and femaleness, seemed the epitome of a fabric whose original power and meaning had been distorted. Historically, lace is a non-gender specific fabric, which was worn by both men and women, largely to indicate wealth, status and culture.

Many of the early designs were of great complexity and influenced interior design and architectural detail. Today lace is primarily associated with lingerie fabric, its rich sense of history lost. I wished to reclaim lace for both men and women, forcing a re-evaluation of the potency and sophistication of early lace designs. I changed the scale, context and interpretation of lace, originating a new technique which allowed me to draw with cut fabrics inlaid into the surface of the work, a process which evokes archaeological excavation and traditional wood block printing. It is effectively a fabric drawing system with allusions to fractals, architecture, ironwork, stained glass and cell structures.

The majority of the early lace work was based on sixteenth-century pattern books. In 1995 I researched the historical lace collection of the Whitworth Art Gallery in Manchester at the invitation of Dr. Jennifer Harris, the collection curator, a project which culminated in the solo exhibition *Material Evidence: Improvisations On A Historical Theme*. I showed six new major works, the largest of which, *Field of Centres* (1996), was 5.50 metres wide. The project highlighted the relationship between the perfect and the imperfect. Antique lace bears the traces of its former life; holes, stains, tears. Fragments of older fabrics could be re-invented and hybridised to create new ideas. In short, I realised that I did not have to be too historically respectful. *Underwater Moonlight* (1997) is one of a series of mid-1990s deconstructed lace works in which bio-morphic references to cell structures become more self-evident. Sections of the original lace designs have been appropriated and re-invented to create an interior cosmic landscape.

At present I am investigating the relationship between the cellular aspect of textile construction and bio-morphic cellular structures. *Twelve Dreams Within The Here And Now* (1998-99) can be viewed as a comment on the implied relationship between culture and cultures. Within both information interrelates, evolves and reconfigures into new visual data. The sequential, circular configurations may be read as both a reference to microscopic lenses and Petrie dishes, the arena within which intellectual and biological information constantly mutates and evolves.

You Are Here (1997), perhaps more than any other work I have made, illustrates the wealth of visual material I research. *You Are Here* is a visual map, that charts influences, both formative and current, which inform my work. The field of the piece refers to a seventeenth-century English

below:
Skeleton Key (1997) (detail)
stitchery, fabric collage, tape, wire, acrylic,
thread on to wood construction
110 x 110 x 4cm

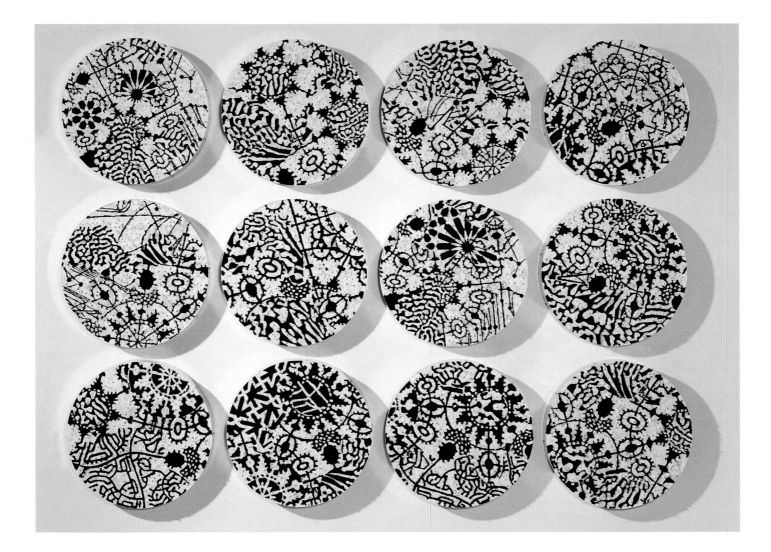

embroidered fabric. Running horizontally across the base is a section of a John Cage score, whose use of chance procedures as a means of generating new ideas has been a constant source of inspiration. The musical river denotes the passage of time. Scattered across the work are references to diagrammatic stitch structures, early writing systems, lace designs, the iconography of Aboriginal painting, Central Asian *suzani* fabrics, Caucasian carpet design, Kazakh felt, pre-history mazes, African textiles, Scandinavian solar discs and the Rorschach ink test. *You Are Here* may be read in any direction; any route across the piece will result in new configurations of idea and image. The title of the work refers to the maps found in most town centres, indicating sites of interest.

Since the advent of Modernism patterning has been regarded as trivial, a view not shared by non-western cultures. As an artist I am interested in the genealogical connections between the source material I collate, the reasons why I associate one idea with another. The adventure is to discern why and make visual sense of the clues amassed. The study of meta-patterns, patterns that connect, reveals much in anthropological terms about our spiritual, cultural and sociological history. Physically, the construction process mirrors the content of the work. Fragments of earlier stages can be glimpsed through veils of colour. *You Are Here* is an instinctive Internet of ideas and references, a visual map charting its own genealogy.

Twelve Dreams Within The Here And Now
(1998-99)
inlaid fabric, marble dust,
painted wooden base with metal edge
12 panels, each 60cm in diameter

Born   1952, Bury, Lancashire

Education and Awards

1972-75	BA (Hons) Textiles, Manchester Polytechnic
1975-77	MA Textiles, Birmingham Polytechnic
1987	Winner of the Creative Concept Award, International Textile Competition, Kyoto
1989	Winner of the Fine Art Award, International Textile Competition, Kyoto
1990	Distinguished Visiting Fellow, British Council, City University, Kyoto
1992	1st Prize Winner, 3rd International Betonac Prize, Belgium

Exhibitions: Solo

1999	*You Are Here*, Bankfield Museum and Piece Hall, Halifax
1999	*Twelve Dreams Within The Here And Now,* Galerie Ra, Amsterdam
1996	*Material Evidence: Improvisations On A Historical Theme*, Whitworth Art Gallery, Manchester (tour)
1994	*A Faint Touch of Fragility*, Galerie Ra, Amsterdam

Exhibitions: Group

1999	*Weaving the World - Contemporary Art of Linear Construction*, Yokohama Museum of Art, Japan
1997	*The Jerwood Prize for Applied Arts – Textiles*, short-list exhibition, Crafts Council Gallery, London
1996	*Recycling – Forms for the Next Century,* Crafts Council Gallery, London (tour)
1996	*Flexible 2 – Pan European Art,* Nederlands Textiel Museum, Tilburg (tour: Poland, England)
1994	*A New Century in Design,* Metropolitan Telen Art Museum, Tokyo (tour)
1993-4	*Flexible 1,* Oberfrankenhalle, Bayreuth, Germany (tour: Holland, Poland, England)
1992	*Out of the Frame,* Crafts Council Gallery, London (tour)

Commissions

1999	Ocean, Music Venue, four related installation works, Hackney, London
1992	Tabor High School, Essex, floor and ceiling installation commissioned by Essex County Council

Professional

1992	Curator, *Restless Shadows*, Japanese fibre exhibition, Goldsmiths College (tour)
1982	Curator, *Fabric and Form*, Crafts Council and British Council
1983-89	Senior Lecturer, Goldsmiths College, University of London

Work in Collection

Contemporary Art Society
Crafts Council, London
Gallery of Western Australia
National Museum of Modern Art, Kyoto, Japan
Powerhouse Museum, Sydney, Australia
Victoria And Albert Museum, London
Whitworth Art Gallery, University of Manchester

Jo Budd

Horizons are the ultimate edge – infinity. These pieces are made to be read in two ways, as a three-dimensional illusion of space, or as a surface with a pattern and rhythm of its own.

left:
Memories of Summer –
Cornfield Series No.17 (1997)
hand-stitched procion and helizarin dyed cotton,
silk and nylon
130 x 38cm

above:
Water on Earth –
Elemental Landscape Series (1999)
hand-stitched, procion dyed silks and cotton
30 x 35cm

The act of making is for me one of trying to understand the world. Since I made my first serious paintings at college I have worked intuitively, being drawn to a subject without knowing why, and it is through the process of exploration in making a piece that I learn what it is that fascinates me as an artist.

With the hindsight of twenty years of working, I can perceive themes which recur and resonate throughout my work. These revolve around a search for balance between contrasts: the large and the small – the overall structure and composition versus surface detail (a contrast I see to some extent as male and female principles, strength versus delicacy), between abstraction and figuration, colour balancing with tone, and two-dimensional surface versus three-dimensional illusion. This last contrast between surface texture and the illusion of space has been an overriding visual concern.

My early oil paintings were highly realistic and observed, usually people in architectural settings. They were about putting humans in perspective. My greatest hero at this point was Vermeer. I admired the mystery and poetry of his interiors as well as his sensuous enjoyment of colour and paint, and the almost palpable atmospheric space, combined with an innate and sublime geometry producing a feeling of inevitability and balance.

I turned to fabric half-way through my fine art degree as a means of 'shedding the weight of art history' and concentrating on formal concerns of composition and colour without the distraction of figuration. Suddenly I could work in an abstract way, with complete freedom, in a medium I felt at home with, but whose constraints limited the range of visual problems I was trying to tackle. Since then my work has gone through many technical changes and discoveries, but I have never felt the need to turn back to paint to express my ideas.

My first ten years of working were spent in a big city. I loved being surrounded by architecture, either new and minimal – large industrial warehouses (order and structure imposed by man) – or old and decaying – derelict sheds or half-demolished buildings (the patterns of nature taking over from man as they decayed). I was mainly concerned with the abstract balancing of surface and colour within the figurative framework of these buildings. The figure was now absent, and I have since realised that if you remove the figure as subject, then the viewer is no longer contemplating another consciousness, but is invited to become one with the artist and to see the world through his/her eyes.

Most of my work has been on a 'heroic' scale (eight to twelve feet). For many reasons I enjoy working large - my works about buildings needed to be big so that you could literally 'look up' to them and realise man's smallness. Colour on a large scale also has a strong and irresistible emotional impact which one can feel in a visceral way. I will never forget standing in front of Rothko's paintings in the Tate Gallery and being overwhelmed by the intensity of emotion that a colour field can generate. Making a large piece predominantly in one colour can have a profound effect on the psyche. Working on a red piece for a long period made me distinctly irritable; working with a large blue piece I found calming.

opposite:
**Enough to Patch a Sailor's Trousers –
Elemental Landscape Series** (1998)
hand-stitched, procion dyed silks and cotton
102 x 33cm

Working in stripes in such a minimal way seems risky but fundamental and inexhaustible. Less is more. Like Bach's *Art of Fugue*, there can be infinite variations on a theme. The turquoise blue in this piece can be read as water or sky – a synergy of heaven and earth.

Colour is the reason for my existence. Throughout my life, distinct colour shifts have occurred as I have moved to different locations. My city years were brown and grey; a brief spell in the country led to green, yellow and blue. The next ten years in a seaside town was my blue, red and multicoloured phase (red for boats and multicoloured for seaside ephemera). This period also coincided with childrearing and a houseful of riotously coloured plastic toys. Now I am back in the countryside. I have not been here long, however, and my first two series of works, *Cornfields – Memories of Summer 97* and *Elemental Landscapes – Earth/Sea/Sky*, have been golden and brown with hints of green (cornfields and earth) and brown and grey (water and mud); it has rained a lot recently!

The colours of the countryside are amazing. I observe them through the seasons and at different times of day, moments which are spectacular or just quietly beautiful, and eventually they are absorbed by the psyche. I now feel I have them in my soul enough to work without photographs or preliminary sketches. Both *Cornfields* and *Elemental Landscapes* capture fleeting moments of light and weather conditions. There are particular times of day which I love: twilight – at dusk and dawn, when the sky can appear divided into incredible horizontal strips of colour, sometimes blazing orange with menacing grey above. Another moment which thrills is before rain when the sky is darker than the land and our normal tonality of light over dark (sky over earth) is reversed. It is as if the world had been turned upside down.

Cornfields and *Elemental Landscapes* were produced like sketches, very spontaneously. They are not representations of actual scenes, but distillations of feelings about landscape. They also contain memories of my years in a studio overlooking the sea – the perpetual horizontal of the horizon, the sea meeting the sky, the same play of light.

The hand-stitching on this piece, though hardly visible from a distance, creates a gentle ripple on the picture surface. The pale blue-grey stiches follow the grain of the fabric. They were a spontaneous addition, reminiscent of ploughed furrows and connecting the earth with the sky.

The space in these works is deliberately ambiguous. You could be looking at earth or water or sky. Sometimes there is what seems like an obvious horizon line, but this can suddenly shift and another line can read as horizon, as in *Enough to Patch a Sailor's Trousers*, or there may be false horizons, as in *Cornfield no.18*, which has no sky. Edges are so fundamental, being the point where one colour meets and interacts with another, soft or hard, contrasting or not in tone or hue; they are a focal point. Horizons are the ultimate edge – infinity. A horizontal can always be read as a horizon and this means of creating space is contrasted in *Elemental Landscapes* with increasingly bold mark-making on the picture surface. These pieces are made to be read in two ways, as a three-dimensional illusion of space, or as a surface with a pattern and rhythm of its own, the minimal stitching enhancing the textural qualities.

Stripes have become symbolic in my work. The city is a place of vertical lines (which predominate In my earlier work), while the country is about horizontals. The insistent horizontals of my current work are often seen within a tall, vertical format – perhaps I am still looking at the country through city eyes?

These two series are also about inner landscapes with other resonances and layers of meaning: the universal principles of natural proportion (the Fibonacci series), DNA, the macrocosm and the microcosm – recurring patterns of nature (fractals). My dyeing procedure now allows the dyes to flow and produce the natural patterns as I print. The less I manipulate the dyes the more they produce the patterns of earth and sky on their own. Working in stripes in such a minimal way seems risky but fundamental and inexhaustible; no wonder so many artists have used them as an underlying structure. Less is more. Like Bach's *Art of Fugue*, and as in nature, I believe there can be infinite variations on a theme, capable of restatement without repetition and with the possibilities of endless discovery and freshness.

My conscious artistic influences contain contrasts – Vermeer's 'detail' and Rothko's 'emptiness', though both are linked by profound emotion and a mood provoking wordless language. The dichotomy between these two symbolises that of my career so far, which has oscillated between the 'narrative' of representation and the 'purity' of abstraction.

Other influences are perhaps more subliminal – though as an artist one cannot help absorbing everything and being a child of one's time – but I should mention Ben Nicholson, Robert Rauschenberg, Kurt Schwitters, Amish quilts, J. S. Bach and my mother, father and sister, all of whom are artists.

Writing about my work I realise that some ideas can be expressed in words, but that ultimately visual language is a wordless one for me. It is, however, a universal one, which many people can feel intuitively; they understand when something 'works' and is 'right'. It is this 'rightness', a feeling of inevitability and of age-old universal principles which speak to us all, on a level of human proportions, balance and harmony, which I am striving for.

Mist and Earth – Elemental Landscape Series
(1998) (detail)
hand-stitched, procion dyed cotton poplin
13 x 10cm

This could be a winter's dawn – a landscape on earth or in the sky.

Fire and Ice –
Elemental Landscape Series
(1998)
hand-sewn, procion dyed silks
and cotton
73 x 45cm

Born   1956, Norwich, Norfolk

Education and Awards
1975-79   BA (Hons) Fine Art, University of Newcastle upon Tyne
1985-88   Northern Arts Awards (five)
1985   Crafts Council Setting-up Grant
1998   Visual Arts Fund Award, Norfolk County Council
1998-99   Two Research Awards, Norwich School of Art and Design

Exhibitions: Solo
1999   *Elemental Landscapes*, King of Hearts Gallery, Norwich
1997   *The Sameling,* Dovenest, Cumbria
1995   Lowestoft Arts Centre, Lowestoft, Suffolk
1985   Northern Centre for Contemporary Arts, Sunderland

Exhibitions: Group
1999   *SAAC Winter Exhibition*, Royal Scottish Academy, Edinburgh
1999   *With Cloth and Needle*, Dockyards Arts Centre, Bermuda
1998-9   *Take 4: New Perspectives on the British Art Quilt*, Whitworth Art Gallery, Manchester (tour)
1997   *Traditions*, Barbican Art Gallery, London (tour)
1994   *What is Embroidery?*, Whitworth Art Gallery, Manchester
1992   *The Art of the Quilt*, Shipley Art Gallery, Gateshead
1992   *Out of the Frame*, Crafts Council Gallery, London (tour)
1990   *Stitched Textiles for Interiors*, Embroiderers' Guild, London and Japan
1989   *The Art of Embroidery*, Aberystwyth Arts Centre (tour)

Commissions
1996   Bedfordshire Hospital NHS Trust
1990   Modern Art Collection, Norwich Castle Museum
1986   Bedfordshire County Education Service

Professional
1994-   Part-time Lecturer, BA Textiles and BA Visual Studies, Norwich School of Art and Design
1986-89   Part-time Lecturer, Suffolk College and Lowestoft College
1998-   Visiting Lecturer at the Royal College of Art, London; Manchester Metropolitan University;
       University of Ulster, Belfast; Nottingham and Nottingham Trent Universities

Work in Collection
       Bank of Switzerland, London
       Embroiderers' Guild, London
       Norwich Castle Museum
       Shipley Art Gallery, Gateshead

Caroline Broadhead

Light, transparent, ghostly dresses whose shadows seem to mimic them, seem like a crowd. A ventilation outlet in the gallery where they were first installed caused them to sway, dance, and become quite animated.

left:
Dress with Black Holes (1998)
wire, cloth, paint
150 x 150 x 30cm

above:
in-crease-de-crease (1999)
net
2m x 7m x 30cm

My recent work has been exploring the play between visibility and invisibility; space and matter; substance and non-substance. There is an element of time: looking back into it; arresting it; an awareness that the work is ephemeral in its nature, often requiring fundamental decisions being made at the time of installation, and the piece not existing as such when the exhibiting period is over.

I have been trying to indicate something more than is there, as a line drawing may imply and suggest volume, space and substance. It is this act of the imagination, the filling in of gaps, that makes up the final piece.

I have always been interested in this engagement with an object. Early smaller pieces were to be handled and explored in a physical way; some changed character in a different position or when they were worn. Later, these pieces grew to cover more of the body and became clothing forms. The reasons I adopted garments as a vehicle for expression were that, firstly, it allowed me to make reference to the whole body or person and not just a fragment; and, secondly, clothing, being familiar and common to all, assured a point of communication. The closeness of the human being is retained in form, proportion, and in the possibility of wearing, or possibly in the memory of it belonging to or having been worn by someone.

I am interested in the borderline between the self and the rest of the world. The garment is a good example of this interface, the facade where we can project our personality, mood, aspirations, where we are capable of disguise, deception and chameleon-like change in different situations. It is the way we all see each other, how we judge and read one another. There is an outside and an inside, a side to be seen by others and a private side. Hence, it is this location that houses fascination, scrutiny, inquiry, analysis and anxiety.

Double Vision works with transparency, seeing through to what is behind. A smaller garment inside takes its form from the outer layer and is therefore distorted. Displayed on a raw plaster plinth, there is reference to classical statues portraying a female ideal. Where then there was solidity, weight and permanence, in my pieces there is frailty, a transient quality, allowing a view to the inside. The definition of an individual, therefore, separates it from everything else, but it can also shift and reshape, overlap and include others, merge with something else.

There has been a focus on the empty garment in both art and craft in recent years, as simultaneous indication of absence and of presence, and this has also been an aspect of some of my own work with garments. However, since 1996, my work has evolved to include the garments' cast shadow as an integral part of the pieces. The shadow also acts as indicator of absence and presence, as well as representing the other side of the personality, the darker side, the negative double of the person.

The first series of small dresses with shadows was called *over my shoulder I-IV*, and when seen altogether, their scale has an unsettling effect, both doll-like and, because the proportions are adult-like, rather sinister. These contradictory qualities are reflective of the references to shadows, which appear both ominous and threatening as well as being seen as the most precious part of the person, in need of protection.

Each of the seven dresses is scaled to give the same shadow on the wall. The closer the dress the sharper the shadow becomes, and the further from the light the darker the dress, so there is a continuity between the dresses and their shadows. The shadow effect is of a pencil drawing which has been erased and attempted again and again.

Tunnel Dress (1999)
wire, silk

Over a series of pieces, I have been gradually giving the shadow more emphasis than the garment that is creating it. There is information in the shadow that makes direct reference to the dress – a floral print, the pattern of the dress lining, or other motifs which have a wider resonance. In *Steppenwolf*, one shadow has a number of daintily coloured rosebuds painted in and the other, a pencil drawing of hair covering the dress shape. In another work, *Ready to Tear*, the shadow falls on to a corner of the room, and the two shadows thus created on the adjoining walls show patterns with contrasting stereotypical feminine associations, the leopard skin print and lace.

Shadows can be seen not only as the result of obstruction of the passage of light, but as mysterious entities with a nature all of their own. The shadow is a powerful symbol, often seen as a manifestation of a person's soul. It is something that both is and is not. It can be blurry at the edges or focused, it can faithfully follow a form – the drawing round of a shadow, getting a likeness, is said to be the origin of painting – or it can loom larger than the object casting it, giving a distorted or unrecognisable view.

I had worked with garments for a number of years and thought I had exhausted the possibilities. So, around 1994, I began to look for something else that could offer me similar opportunities for the expression of ideas. During a period of research, I began to explore shadows in a number of different ways: by drawing (several were timed drawings of the shadows of a chair as the sun moved round, getting multiple images); by taking photographs (some of my own shadow on different surfaces, early morning or noontime shadows); by reading (I was struck by the role of Dante's shadow in *The Divine Comedy*, when the shadowless dead souls are taken aback as the sun comes up to reveal Dante as the only living person in purgatory). I found that this new information invigorated my ideas about the garment. It was when the garment and the shadow worked together that there was room for ideas about the individual, the separation or integration of different parts of the psyche.

When I work into the shadow I am interested in its connection to the surroundings, in the way it impinges upon the wall or the surface. There is a sense of being grounded, of belonging.

The Waiting Game was a collaborative piece with choreographer, Angela Woodhouse, at Upnor Castle in Kent. This English Heritage building is an Elizabethan garrison on the River Medway, which was an important lookout post for enemy ships coming up the river. The dance performance was a response to the history of the place, the buildings themselves and the surroundings. I made a number of white garments; some were worn by the dancers, and others were tucked away in corners, lurking in small places, where you happened upon them. I saw these as shadows from the past, giving form to the ghostly presences that exist in these old buildings. One dress was made to fit one of the rooms, giving a feeling of being tethered to the place, not allowed to leave, being defined by and merging with the fabric of the building. Here, to see this part of the dance, the audience had to walk into the room and tread on the dancer's white linen dress. In this work I wished to create a sense of invasion of someone else's territory, not in a mighty, aggressive, warlike way, but suggesting the sense of discomfort or unease when this is experienced on a personal level.

In Vienna I mapped out the real patch of sunlight (right). Having spent two days threading the window and the floor, I had to wait a week for the overcast weather to clear until the magical moment when the sun aligned itself with my cage of threads.

Still Light (1999)
elastic, talc
3 x 7 x 2m

in-crease-de-crease is a line of dresses made of fine net. The centre one follows the proportions of a person and, being the same colour as the walls it hangs in front of, becomes confused with its own shadow, while the outer ones become progressively larger or smaller on either side and gradually increase in colour to blue or red. The extremes become strange distortions of the middle piece. When I conceived this work I was thinking of the way we see ourselves as the centre of the space we occupy – the physical mass of our bodies, and also of the invisible territory outside of our bodies that we claim as ours.

Still Light is the first piece I have made where there is no reference to the individual, and represents a significant development for me. The wall, another boundary that defines what is me, what is mine and what is not, what is something else, is penetrated by a shaft of light. The elastic lines map out a space on the floor, separating it off, making the light patch an impenetrable area. I liked the idea of taking a three-dimensional 'photograph', a frozen moment in time. It is both terrifying and reassuring to know that the world will keep turning, time will keep moving on.

Having worked with the idea of a cast shadow, *Still Light* was a look at the reverse, a natural light projection through a window. It is a view that is immediately familiar, evocative, even melancholic. Even though it is obvious it speaks of just one moment; the sun or moon's path is constantly changing; the effect is one of timelessness.

The dress, or person, combines with the architecture, rooted to the spot. This was one of a number of garments that were located at Upnor Castle, Kent

above:
from **The Waiting Game** (1997)
in collaboration with Angela Woodhouse
at Upnor Castle, Kent
linen
130cm x 10m x 10m

Born 1950, Leeds, Yorkshire

Education and Awards

1969-72 Jewellery Design, Central School of Art and Design
1997 Winner of the Jerwood Prize for Applied Arts: Textiles

Exhibitions: Solo

1999 *Bodyscape: Caroline Broadhead*, Angel Row Gallery, Nottingham (tour)

Exhibitions: Group

1999 *Weaving the World,* Yokohama Museum of Art, Japan
1998 *Addressing the Century, 100 Years of Art and Fashion*, Hayward Gallery, London (tour)
1998 *Beyond Material,* Oriel Mostyn Gallery, Llandudno (tour)
1998 *Tempered,* Fabrica, Brighton
1996 *Under Construction*, Crafts Council Gallery, London (tour)
1993 *On the Edge*, Crafts Council Gallery, London (tour)
1990 *Three Ways of Seeing,* retrospective with Fred Baier and Richard Slee, Crafts Council Gallery, London
1986 *Conceptual Clothing,* Ikon Gallery, Birmingham (tour)

Performances

1997 *The Waiting Game*, collaboration with Angela Woodhouse, Upnor Castle, Kent
1995 *Unlaced Grace*, collaboration with Clare Russ, Mill Arts Centre, Banbury

Professional

1998 Artist-in-Residence, Vienna, Austria
1999, 1997 Internationale Sommerakademie, Salzburg, Austria
1996- Goldsmiths College, University of London, BA (Hons) Textiles
1986- University of Middlesex, BA (Hons) Jewellery

Publications

1999 *Bodyscape: Caroline Broadhead* (Angel Row Gallery, Nottingham)
1999 Michael Raeburn*, 50 Years of British Creativity* (London, Thames and Hudson)
1998 *Addressing the Century, 100 Years of Art and Fashion* (London, Hayward Gallery)
1998 Pamela Johnson (ed.)*, Ideas in the Making, Practice into Theory* (Crafts Council and University of East Anglia)
1992 Chloe Colchester, *The New Textiles* (London, Thames & Hudson)
1990 John Houston, *Caroline Broadhead in Studio* (London, Bellew Publishing and Crafts Council)
1985 Peter Dormer & Ralph Turner, *The New Jewellery* (London, Thames and Hudson)

Work in Collection

Crafts Council, London
Stedelijk Museum, Amsterdam
Crafts Board of Australia Council, Sydney, Australia
Museum of Modern Art, Kyoto

Shelly Goldsmith

In some of my most recent tapestries the warp has assumed an unlikely importance. The skeleton of the piece, it has become dominant. I have pulled or forced the warp through the tapestry weave or left it hanging at the edges, alluding to tears, leaks or waterfalls. No longer flat pieces, these new works interact with space beyond the wall and open up the possibility of creating shadows and the illusion of different scales.

left:
Bathymetric – The Longest River IV (1999) (detail)
tapestry, cotton and nylon monofilament
23 x 98cm

right:
Slowly Seeping (1999)
tapestry, cotton and silk
66 x 53 x 10cm

My work does not hit you in the face. Each piece resembles a word in a sentence formed to express my ideas, offering up clues for discovery. Like the very process I use to make the work, the viewing of it demands time, time to allow the meaning to unravel. I am interested in the woven image, constructed and de-constructed images, in their capacity to tell a story and to express thought. What I produce is a synthesis of thoughts, gut reactions and hard labour!

My work has always expressed a fascination with the making of the world, the making of us? From a very early age I was concerned with how things came about, and where they went. I believe that as visual artists we truly have only one issue which we spend our lives searching to understand, to make sense of through a multitude of guises.

Over the years I have come to understand a common thread in the work I have produced, which my current work strongly reflects. A recent trip to Tokyo introduced me to the eastern approach to medicine. This has engendered an interest in the notion of the three states of water (solid, liquid and gas) and their subsequent states of mutation. My fascination with global rhythms and continuous cycles has led me to explore the power of the tides and the influence of the moon and the sun on all global liquids. I have looked at the physical and the scientific implications of the flow of water on both the earth and in the body. I have formulated a fictitious human landscape.

My current focus of interest is the never-ending ecosystem which acts as a metaphor for life and death — for the things that we do not have much control over! I have considered, for example, a glass of water after it has passed the lips. Our bodies are composed mainly of water and since water travels constantly over the earth we must be linked to everything else on earth? There are some things from which you cannot escape.

The parallel tasks of drawing and making form the basis of my work. The exploration of ideas is always carried out initially through a form of drawing. The 'making' is an involvement with techniques such as weaving, dyeing and photography etc. Tapestry is the predominant medium in which I choose to expand these ideas, but related media are also important at times. With its rich history, textiles offers a wealth of understanding. We all have a relationship with, and ideas about, the textiles by which we are surrounded, whether they be domestic, fashion or historical objects.

The marriage of fibres and approaches can set up a dialogue. A densely hand-woven tapestry may sit next to an industrially manufactured sheer silk. In *Monsoon Capital*, for example, the monsoon map of the world is hand-woven as a tapestry funnel whose warp threads flow through a second, translucent silk funnel, heat transfer-printed with the image of my own rib cage.

This large format tapestry consists of three images placed side by side. In an attempt to suggest repetition, a slither of blue and red 'bottle' shapes appears on the left edge. If both edges of the tapestry were pulled together, the image would form a continuous loop.

Rhythm of Land (1992)
tapestry, cotton, wool and silk
150 x 200cm

I have a love-hate relationship with the medium of tapestry, which creates an on-going debate with the boundaries that define the technique. During my formative years after leaving college, when I was exploring my territory and developing a visual language, I was known to deface it, to cut up lengths of lovingly woven tapestry, to bleach out large sections of colour and then use my own hair to sew it all back together again. All of this in an effort to find an appropriate answer to a visual question.

And, yet, the craft of tapestry is very important to me. It is a challenging medium which demands a great investment of time and foresight. "You must be so patient!", I hear time and time again, but it is not about patience, it is more to do with a commitment to getting it right. It is difficult to maintain the balance between being prepared to make and remake, if necessary, in order to resolve a piece, and at the same time retaining the spontaneity and excitement inherent in the original concept. However, I am not overly concerned with the finer points of technique, with straight edges or 'dovetail linking' but, as with drawing, once you have learned the craft, you drop a few techniques and add some of your own. Skill and experience is what you need to work unselfconsciously. These free me to manipulate the materials and get them to do what I want them to.

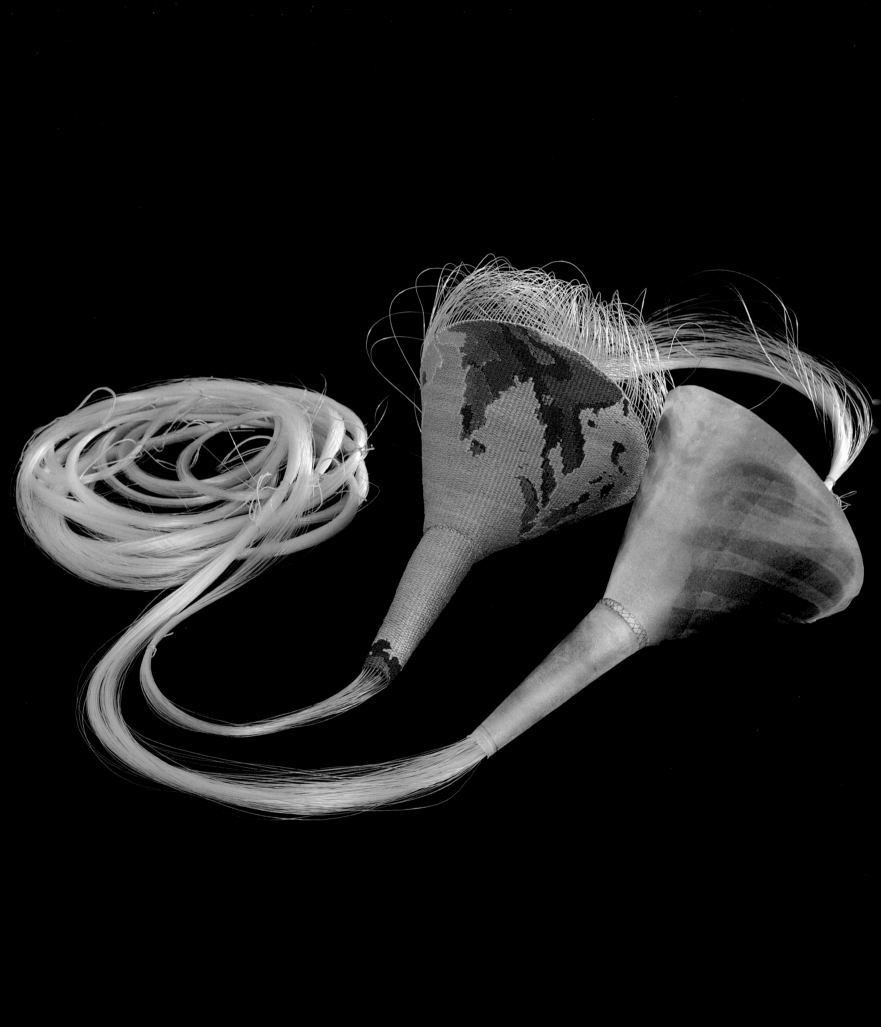

This woven funnel (left) was constructed slowly over time. The work involved stages of deliberation, weaving and unweaving. An x-ray of my rib cage was very quickly (in just 18 seconds) heat-transferred on to sheer silk to create the second funnel. The central core of the first funnel, the warp, passes through the centre of the second funnel.

There is a fundamental relationship between skill and content. I continue to find tapestry a challenging and fascinating medium. It satisfies my desire to create something out of a pile of threads, scooped up off my studio floor. The principle of tapestry weaving necessitates the building up of the image from the bottom to the top. This assures the integration of image within the structure. The image penetrates the surface, goes all the way through.

The rhythmic process of hand weaving successfully mimics the rhythms of life which inspired me to create in the first place. Woven cloth is built up from warp and weft, a simple and sturdy structure. Yet, how easily this can disintegrate again. This impression of fragility, however, is misleading for tapestries can and have survived centuries. Ample testimony to this can be found in the ancient textiles preserved in museum collections around the world. These collections have fed and inspired me, though my work is also informed by science, mainstream contemporary art, film and music.

Unlike the traditional approach, where designs or 'cartoons' are translated into tapestry by a team of weavers, my practice is a solitary undertaking. Rarely do I choose a drawing to transcribe literally, since such an approach would leave me little opportunity for creative development in the making of the piece. I just know that I would get bored! The process of weaving is for me a decision-making experience where issues are explored. This process of discovery through manipulating materials consolidates my ideas and allows me to reject inappropriate or unrealistic approaches. I learn about the essence of the idea, how to translate it and the potential of the materials. Each piece is like a sketch with a series of complex decisions to be made along the way.

The way in which I approach my work has changed dramatically over the years, as has the manner in which it is shown. In the early part of my career I produced tapestries that worked with image and colour, almost in the painting tradition. Intrigued by the idea of the drawn line in tapestry I was determined to 'draw' with the same fluidity in the cloth as I did on paper. Concerned with the translation of a mark through the tapestry medium, I worked with the visual qualities of different yarns and the illusion of layering. I devoted months and months to weaving some of the biggest pieces I have made to date.

A reassessment of materials and their relative qualities has caused me to introduce nylon monofilament thread. I use this to weave semi-transparent cloth that does not attempt to hide the opaque white cotton warp. Used as a warp thread it forms a slippery transparent interior to the cloth. The relationship between transparency and opacity, solid and fluid begins to become apparent.

Trained in the traditional French *Gobelin* technique, I was taught that tapestries were hung on the wall, that the warp threads were a structural necessity but were not to be seen. My recent work has challenged this dictum. The tapestries have become tiny while the warp has become huge, and they are very often free-standing. The urge to liberate the tapestry from the wall has become a recurring feature of my work. I would find myself wrapping objects with image-based cloth or placing tapestry slithers in glass domes in site-specific installations.

Monsoon Capital (1999)
tapestry, silk, nylon monofilament
23 x 23 x 215cm

Finally, these experiments resulted in a series of tapestries sandwiched between oval sheets of thin glass which were held with pincers at right angles to the wall. The pieces continued to reflect my fascination with image and cloth, but could be viewed from the front and the back, revealing what would not normally be seen.

In some of my most recent work the warp has assumed an unlikely importance. The skeleton of the piece, it has become dominant. I have pulled or forced the warp through the tapestry weave or left it hanging at the edges, alluding to tears, leaks or waterfalls. No longer flat pieces, these new works interact with space beyond the wall and open up the possibility of creating shadows and the illusion of different scales.

Travel has also been influential. Once, crossing the globe on a flight from London to Australia, a panorama of oceans, lagoons, lakes and pools was revealed below me. During my stay in Australia I discovered that a water-hole will be charted on a map if it has evidence of water at least once in ten years! I found myself pondering once again the implications of the transference of water on the planet!

This double-sided crescent-shaped tapestry *(opposite page)* is sandwiched between thin glass. With woven imagery that suggests the pelvis or an estuary, the warp threads tumble like a waterfall.

right:
Gush Out (1996)
tapestry, cotton and nylon monofilament, glass and metal pincers
250 x 35 x 75cm

Born   1962, Corringham, Essex

Education and Awards

1982-85	BA (Hons) Textiles, West Surrey College of Art and Design, Farnham
1985-87	MA Tapestry, Royal College of Art
1989	Greater London Arts Grant
1989	Crafts Council Setting-up Grant
1995	Winner of Parnel Prize, Royal Overseas League
1998	British Council Travel Award

Exhibitions: Solo

1999	*Dew Point*, Gallery Aoyama, Tokyo (tour: UK, Spain)
1997	*Flow*, Barbican Art Gallery, London
1995	*L Space*, Canberra School of Art, Australia
1992	*Vital Spark*, Gainsborough's House, Suffolk

Exhibitions: Group

1998	*British Art Now – 98*, Axis Gallery, Tokyo
1998	*The British Tapestry Triennial*, Harley Gallery, Nottinghamshire
1998	*Itnet – 4: Tapestries 40/100 on the Internet*, http://www.alaska.net/~itnet/
1998	*Harmony – American Tapestry Biennial II*, Fernbank Museum of Natural History, Atlanta
1998	*Life Force*, Art Gallery, Bury St Edmunds
1996	*The Woven Image*, Contemporary British Tapestry, Barbican Art Gallery, London (tour)
1995	*The British Tapestry Triennial*, Harley Gallery, Nottinghamshire
1995	*Unlaced Grace*, Southampton Art Gallery (tour)
1994	*Pitch*, site-specific installation at Trinity Buoy Wharf, London Docklands
1990	*New British Textile Art*, Ninonbashi Takashimaya Department Store Gallery, Tokyo
1989-90	*British Tapestry*, British and Hungarian tour
1988-9	*World Tapestry Today*, international touring exhibition

Commissions

1998	The River and Rowing Museum, Henley (David Chipperfield Architects)
1989	Lewis Moberly Design Group

Professional

1991-	Course Leader and Founder, BA (Hons) Textile Art, Winchester School of Art
1998	NOPE Studios, Tokyo
1996	National College of Art and Design, Oslo
1995	Artist-in-Residence, Canberra School of Art

Work in Collection

Victoria and Albert Museum, London

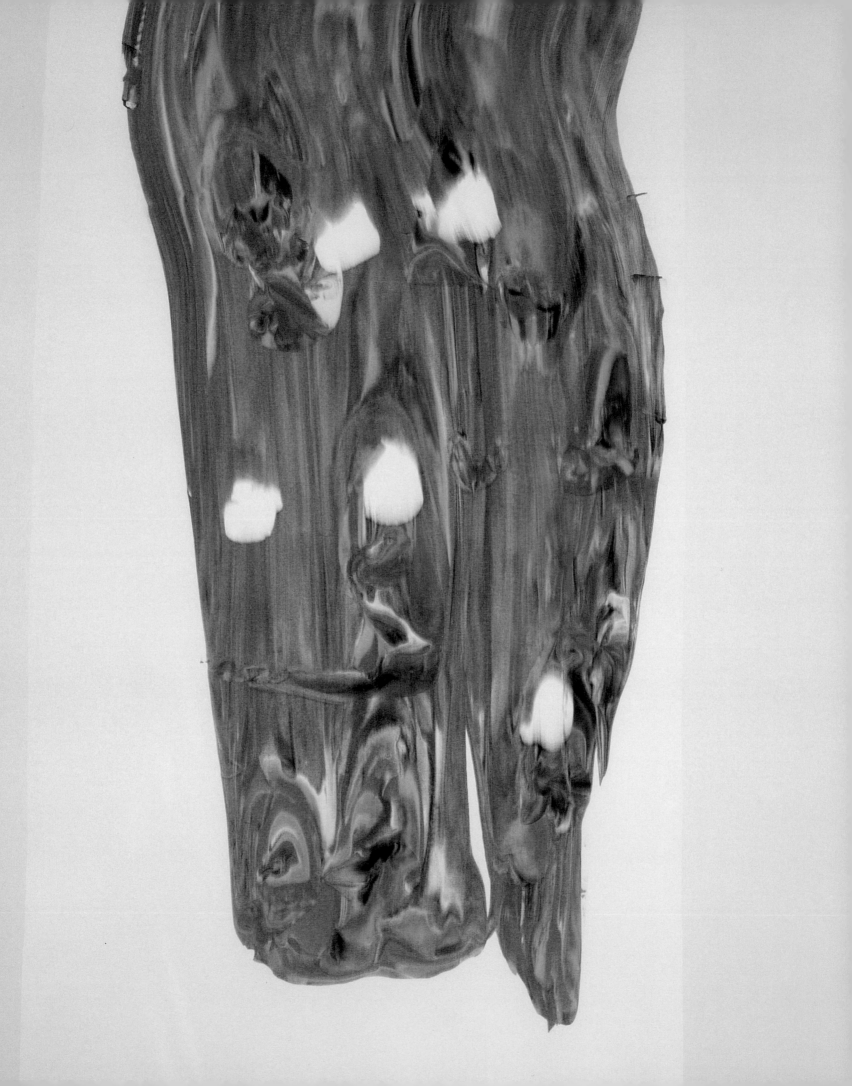

Rushton Aust

Colour has a particular potency for me. Initially, it was the sheer visual and emotional impact of confronting colour; the moment of impact, the 'hit' almost lifts me from the ground.

left:
Untitled (1998) (detail)
squeegeed pigment on polyester
1.75 x 2m

above:
Part of an ongoing series of interrelated pieces (1992-)
printed and painted textile
from 6.5m x 1m to 1.5m x 10cm

I make painted and printed one-off textile pieces using dyes and silk-screen printing materials that are normally used in the manufacture of commercially printed and dyed fabrics.

The roots of my work go back to the period when I was studying textile design at Derby Lonsdale College of Higher Education. As it became apparent to me, and others, that I did not have the abilities nor the inclination necessary for generating designs on paper for fashion or interiors, I was fortunate to be supported and encouraged to pursue my interest in the materials and processes related to industrially produced textiles.

I became fascinated with fabric, and aware of its origins as a fibre, with the forming of thread and the diverse fabric structures that are possible, although it was the subtle and infinite shifts in the characteristics of plain woven cloth which interested me most. The sounds also captured my imagination: the grunt of cotton as it is cut with scissors, the screams of torn silk, and the thwack and whistle of a squeegee across a taut nylon screen mesh. I learnt that textiles could be transparent, reflective, heavy, dense and that they can be manipulated to make three-dimensional forms, qualities which later became significant in the work I made.

Cotton drill, power drill, seed drill. Essential drill bits.

Flexible, amenable, sensuous, close and familiar, cloth reflects the essential functions in human lives, has relationships with the individual, with communities and cultures, which it describes and defines. It carries the symbolism. Our understanding of fabric is instinctive; cloth is so familiar that it is hardly seen. This universality appeals to me as a maker of things. These aspects underpin and reinforce my interest in and research into textiles. The colouring and marking of textile material led me to an interest in hand-dyeing and screen-printing.

Colour has a particular potency for me. Initially, it was the sheer visual and emotional impact of confronting colour; the moment of impact, the 'hit' almost lifts me from the ground. Later, I sought information relating to colour theory and colour symbolism, finding books, reading. Who would have believed it – someone who left school with one 'O' level?

I look for colour unconsciously, for the relation of one colour to another, for proportion. Searching for, looking at and experiencing colour has no apparent purpose, no tangible outcome; there are no goals scored after this running around. I run to see nonetheless.

During a two-year art foundation course I instinctively made a shift from ceramics to painting and textiles, aware of the increased potential of scale and colour. In retrospect what would prove to be pivotal decisions were made instinctively and, at the time, in a quite arbitrary manner. I found the painting studio stifling and restrictive in numerous ways (it was a male domain where 'girls' were invited in. I flinched instinctively and found the door). I escaped to a large, empty room with two big rubber-faced tables and a cupboard containing fabric printing pigments – the textile printing studio. I had found my place, a place to explore the materials and language of textiles.

Untitled (1997)
doubled-sided printed cotton pieces
2.5m x 20cm

Art galleries were an important source of colour and of the 'hit' from early on. The art gallery also had other resonances allied to an earlier experience of architecture. The barn – huge, made of concrete sections, metal and wood, a functional, pure and brutal architecture in relation to its earthy, natural surroundings. Bright, coloured plant – parked and waiting – odd to call it 'plant'. Metal, industrial, it is the antithesis of 'plant'. Of all the large buildings and structures of my childhood, including the church and school, the barn was the place I really responded to. It was the only place for proper contemplation and meditation, a place to think.

Graduating from an MA in printed textiles I became involved in relatively conventional textile design and consultancy, although I began to realise that a fuller engagement with textile materials and printing processes was necessary. In printing there is a point where the fabric is concealed, where the stencil and screen conspire to obscure the cloth, where experience and understanding, of materials and of temperature, where consistency of colour and stencil, friction from the fabric surface, the density and tension of the mesh, the linearity of the squeegee blade, are all manifest. That moment, where the coalition of these factors is revealed as the mesh screen is prised from the fabric surface, is incredibly intense.

Commission by Coca-Cola Schweppes
one of seven pieces in the series (1994)
printed fabric
3m x 60cm

With commissioned work, different associations and dialogues are essential to the success of a project. Agents form a creative conduit between commissioner, architects and artist: others involved in the installation and practical aspects of the commissioning process also make a crucial contribution. I source suitable fabrics and other materials and develop processes that are appropriate for use in public spaces. Issues around cleaning, durability, site maintenance and compliance with fire regulations are fundamental considerations.

The materials and methods I chose acted as a catalyst which led me to consider the associated contexts and to begin to explore the definitions and conventions that are associated with 'textile'. I am a child spinning in one of my mother's summer cotton dresses, newly unpacked from winter hibernation, crisp, cool, exotic, the sensation of cloth in animation. Could that skirt spin!

I have a particular interest in edges and in things that sit on the periphery, the dilemmas, energies and frictions which are generated at an edge. I identify, and have an affinity, with communities, cultures and individuals that site themselves or operate at the margins. This curiosity with the edge is evident in the work I make, in the formal visual elements of the work and in the experience of scanning the landscape, in walking and tracing edges.

Much of my more recent work has been made to commission and has involved creating pieces for interiors, often working with architects and publicly funded bodies. Collaboration has thus become an essential feature of the work which I make and can take several different forms. With commissioned work different associations and dialogues are essential to the success of a project; it involves agents – individuals connected to public or corporate bodies – forming a creative conduit between commissioner, architects and artist. I regard others involved in the installation and practical aspects of the commissioning process as making a positive and crucial contribution. I source suitable fabrics and other materials and develop processes that are appropriate for use in public spaces. Issues around cleaning, durability, site maintenance and compliance with fire regulations are fundamental considerations. Recent collaborative projects have involved schools and hospitals, engaging groups and communities in a number of ways to create a textile work for their immediate environment. Practical, taught workshops are often a component, and I have become increasingly interested in working with other communities in this way.

There are many aspects to my textile practice. I make experimental textile work for exhibition nationally and internationally, which encourages collectors and other bodies to commission work. More recently I have organised and engaged in specialist fabric printing workshops, and have found the process of dialogue and negotiation an important aspect of extending my practice. Related to this is my involvement in teaching in the textile study area of the Department of Visual Arts at Goldsmiths College, London.

Often the starting-point for the speculative textile pieces I make is a collection of drawings, collages and/or photographs. These are generated in response to landscape, real or imagined, and are an essential source. The dilemmas of urban, industrial landscape in relation to the natural and organic are an ongoing concern. I record and collect objects from my immediate urban environment – scraps of found colour, text and other graphic elements describing my surroundings and culture. These inform the colour, proportion and shape of a particular piece, subsumed, manipulated and developed through drawing, photography and, more recently, by computer and the use of film.

The variety of movement and pace experienced by different forms of transport – ceaselessly shifting, creating distance and different focal points, animated by my own movement – is also an influence. I have a memory of the fleeting landscape viewed from a red Ford 'D' series 'custom cab', and a sense of velocity experienced from the window of the *shinkansen* in Japan, which have informed recent work.

Part of the process of making work is the organisation of an appropriate space, where the surroundings and ambience allow visual imagination and focus, a spiritual space, often a quiet place. My initial motivation and ambition was fuelled by the modern gallery space, white, light and quiet. The impression of the architectural experience had significant resonance for me. The contents may have impact, but the gallery space itself was the draw. Contemporary urban architecture, especially the interior, is an ongoing preoccupation – the concrete barn tempered by the vibration of movement through the landscape.

Untitled (1998)
squeegeed pigment on polyester
1.75 x 2m

Born   1958, Oxford

Education and Awards

1976-79   Diploma in Textile Design, Derby Lonsdale College of Higher Education
1979-81   MA Printed Textiles, Royal College of Art
            Crafts Council Setting-up Grant

Exhibitions: Solo

1990-1   Sue Williams Gallery, London
1990   Contemporary Applied Arts, London

Exhibitions: Group

1997   *The Jerwood Prize for Applied Arts: Textiles*, short-list exhibition, Crafts Council Gallery, London
1996-8   *Objects of our Time*, Crafts Council Gallery, London (tour)
1996   *Under Construction*, Crafts Council Gallery, London (tour)
1996   *The Artist's Journey*, Bury St Edmunds Art Gallery
1995   *8th Triennale of Tapestry,* Central Museum of Textiles, Lodz, Poland (Bronze Medal)
1993-4   *Flexible 1 – Pan-European Art,* Oberfrankenhalle, Bayreuth, Germany (tour: Holland, Poland, England)
1994   *Colour into Cloth*, Crafts Council Gallery, London (tour)
1993   *Rushton Aust and Tom Dixon,* Oriel Gallery, Cardiff
1992   *Contemporary Textiles*, Bonington Gallery, Nottingham Trent University
1991-2   *Alison Britton en Andere Britten*, Gallery Kapelhuis, Amsterdam, Netherlands
1990-1   *Textile Arts – Multicultural Traditions*, Leicester City Gallery (tour)
1988-9   *Contemporary British Crafts,* National Museum of Modern Art, Kyoto; National Museum of Modern Art, Tokyo

Commissions

1998   Nottingham Castle Museum
1998   Seaton Sluice First School, Northumberland, Community Arts Project
1997   Museum of Science and Industry in Manchester
1997   Hayward Gallery Café – installation with students from Goldsmiths College
1996   Norfolk and Norwich Healthcare Trust – made in collaboration with staff and patients of St Stephens Hospital, Norwich
1994   Coca-Cola UK

Professional

1994-   Part-time Lecturer in Textile Studies, Goldsmiths College, University of London

Work in Collection

            Crafts Council, London
            Glasgow City Council
            Museum of Modern Art, Tokyo
            Stedelijk Museum, Amsterdam
            Contemporary Art Society, Tate Gallery, London

Lesley Mitchison

What fascinates me most about the corset is its history in fabric and in memory; the complicated structure and attention to detail reflected in its many faceted layers and lacings. I have interpreted it through woven structures such as double, triple and even quadruple cloths.

Decadence 1991
woven, embroidered and assembled
cotton, silk, polyester yarns,
brass wire and polyester boning
69 x 112cm

My solo exhibition *A Scrutiny of Constraint*, which toured the UK between 1991 and 1993, was the culmination of a year-long residency at Derby University and a previous appointment at Cumbria College of Art as a Teaching Fellow. It was also a major turning-point in my career as a practising artist as it offered an opportunity to break away from previous modes of working.

As a student my preoccupation had been with the weaving process itself, producing flat woven lengths concerned with constructional techniques. Now the woven fabrics were altered as soon as they came off the loom, nipped into and shaped to look like stray panels from full-length female corsets. The subtlety of neutral tones and monochrome colour was the only association left from my time at college in Farnham.

The source and inspiration for this body of work came from underwear, particularly the corset. I was very interested in the social implications of the corset image as it has often been used as a metaphor to convey the position of women and to deal with issues of gender. As my research developed I realised that what fascinated me most about the corset was its history in fabric and in memory, and the complicated structure and attention to detail reflected in its many faceted layers and lacings. It is probably because of this complicated structure that I interpreted it through woven structures such as double, triple and, occasionally, quadruple cloths. I enjoy the complexity of threading up the loom when great concentration is required.

My research for the work in *A Scrutiny of Constraint* involved visits to various textile museums such as the Symington collection of corsets in Leicester and the Museum of Costume at Camphill House in Glasgow. Cross-referencing the form of the corset involved looking at other sources of visual information, such as Italian landscape, where the structure of the hills and fields was reminiscent of the tucks and folds and lines of stitching found in corset construction. Laterally thinking through ideas is an integral part of the way I develop visual research.

Drawing and using a sketchbook are essential to me in recording and exploring qualities of surface, form and texture. The process of drawing and painting is also a time for reflection. I do not always know exactly what I want to make. Often, in the initial stages of making, it is more a feeling or an idea about structure that I wish to explore. I believe that the qualities and essence of one's work are arrived at through the absorption of a variety of sources, and through an underlying questioning. There are inevitably times of great doubt, but I always know that I will get there in the end.

How I work is usually determined by the individual projects or exhibitions with which I am involved. Deadlines help to focus my time between teaching, doing my own work and bringing up a young family. Essentially, the content of the work is a personal exploration of ideas and issues that I want to put forward. *Sway Back* was commissioned for an exhibition entitled *Unlaced Grace*, which commemorated the closing down of the Spencer corset factory in Banbury, Oxford. It was a group show co-ordinated by Caroline Broadhead, and presented an opportunity for me to explore the corset in a new and different context and not to view it only as a vehicle dealing with gender, women's issues or sex.

A work about memory in clothing and the vulnerability of textile fibres and fabrics, inspired by the collection of paper garments from the Second World War in the Conservation Collection at the War Memorial Museum in Canberra, Australia.

Mend and Make Do II (1997)
woven, printed (devoré), embroidered and assembled
silk, cotton, polyester yarns
74 x 50 x 10cm

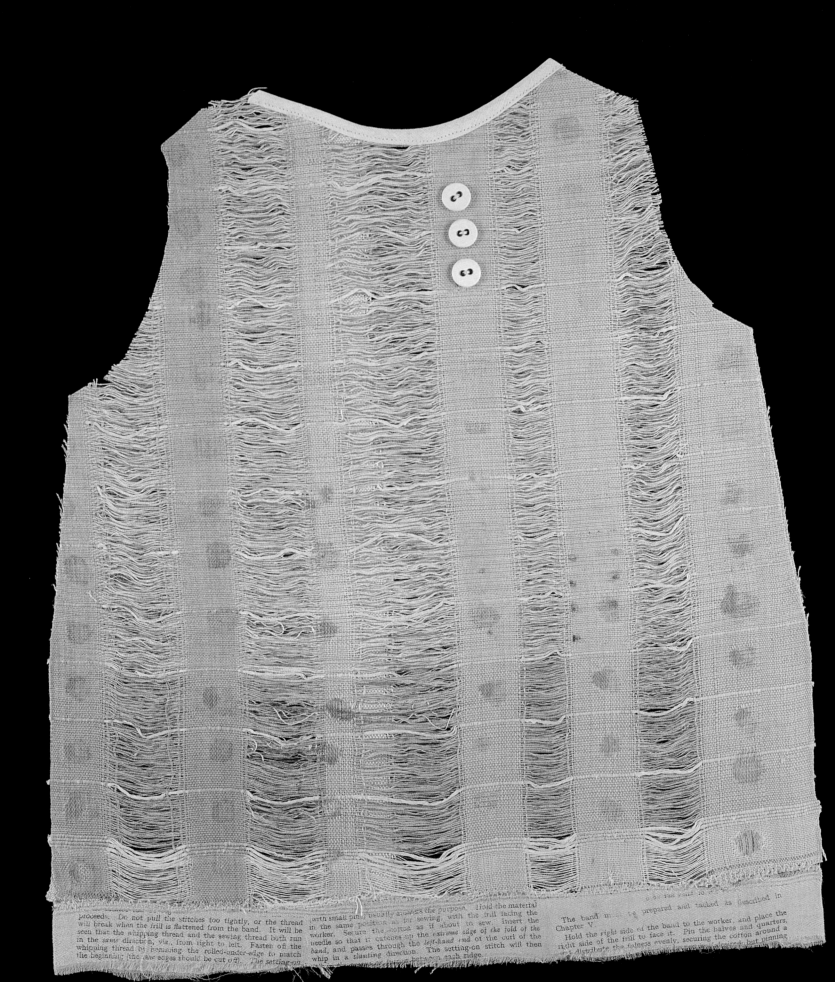

proceeds. Do not pull the stitches too tightly, or the thread will break when the frill is flattened from the band. It will be seen that the whipping thread and the sewing thread both run in the *same* direction, viz., from right to left. Fasten off the whipping thread by hemming the rolled-under-edge to match the beginning (the raw edges should be cut off). The setting-on

with small pins, usually answers the purpose. Hold the material in the same position as for sewing, with the frill facing the worker. Secure the cotton as if about to sew, insert the needle so that it catches on the *extreme edge of the fold of the band*, and passes through the *left-hand end* of the curl of the whip in a *slanting direction*. The setting-on stitch will then

The band must be prepared and tacked as described in Chapter V

Hold the *right* side of the band to the worker, and place the right side of the frill to face it. Pin the halves and quarters, and distribute the fulness evenly, securing the cotton around a

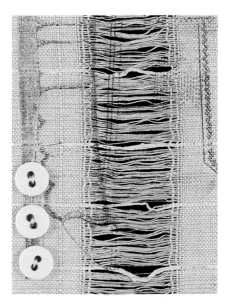

A fallen hem, a tired and worn seam, a missing button or a lovingly darned and repaired tear are qualities that I am always looking out for. I admire the care that has been taken in repairing, mending and truly recycling fabrics. The resourcefulness of past generations should not be forgotten.

left and above:
Making Clothes for Children I (1998)
woven and heat transfer printed cotton, polyester, paper, silk yarns
36 x 32cm

'Sway back' is a medical term for curvature of the spine. The two corset shapes hover and almost touch. The placing of one similar, but not identical, form on top of another refers to the way the body changes through time, and posture through ailment, and echoes the repetition of making. There are subtle differences in the twist of each corset shape. The name labels stitched on to the outside of each piece serve to emphasise the personal involvement of the medical corset makers with their patients. This work was the beginning of an exploration of three-dimensional form, making structures I imagined I could walk around.

In 1994 I was invited to undertake a three-month residency at the Australian National University in Canberra, an intense period of teaching, lecturing and producing new work. Most of the work undertaken at this time was in the form of maquettes, which I often use to explore possibilities for form and structure. I could not weave for part of the residency, which provided a perfect opportunity for more exploratory drawing and sampling. I was fascinated by the Australian flora and fauna, which seemed so exotic but whose shapes reminded me of the bustles and crinolines from my earlier research.

I had an opportunity to visit the conservation centre at the War Memorial Museum in Canberra (which houses the main collection of wartime memorabilia) and was shown a collection of paper garments and, more significantly, the *Changi* quilts. These items evoked a sense of transient memory, the passing of time, fragility, and vulnerability, which derived from the particular circumstances and time of their making.

They were made in internment camps in Singapore by women civilian prisoners of war. Three quilts were made in total, one for each of the British, Australian and Japanese Red Cross, in the hope that they might be taken to the hospital in the military camp. The making of the quilts stemmed from the need to circumvent Japanese restrictions on communication between the military and civilian camps; their most important function was the identification of women who were still alive. The quilts were patched together from materials such as sugar bags and fragments of clothing, and were both machine and hand sewn.

These textiles and their associations had a profound influence on the direction of my work. My interest in fabric construction was evolving alongside an interest in the making of clothes and the changes effected by wear and time. The body of new work which grew out of these concerns coincided with an invitation to participate in the exhibition *Revelation – textile artists addressing issues*. Curated by Lesley Millar, the exhibition presented contemporary textile art in a broad and challenging context. It toured to the Museum of Modern Art in Kyoto, Japan, where I was invited to lecture and to host workshops. This was an invaluable experience, and the challenge of translating my thoughts and ideas into another language also served to reaffirm the direction which my work was taking.

Mend and Make Do 1 and 11 express ideas about the fragility of textile fabrics through the process of weaving a structure and then proceeding to burn away the surface to create shadow-like images. This process is called *devoré*. It involves screen-printing a chemical solution on to fabric which, when heated, burns away the cellulose fibres (plant-based fibres) leaving other fibres intact. In my case the structure of the woven cloth is imperative.

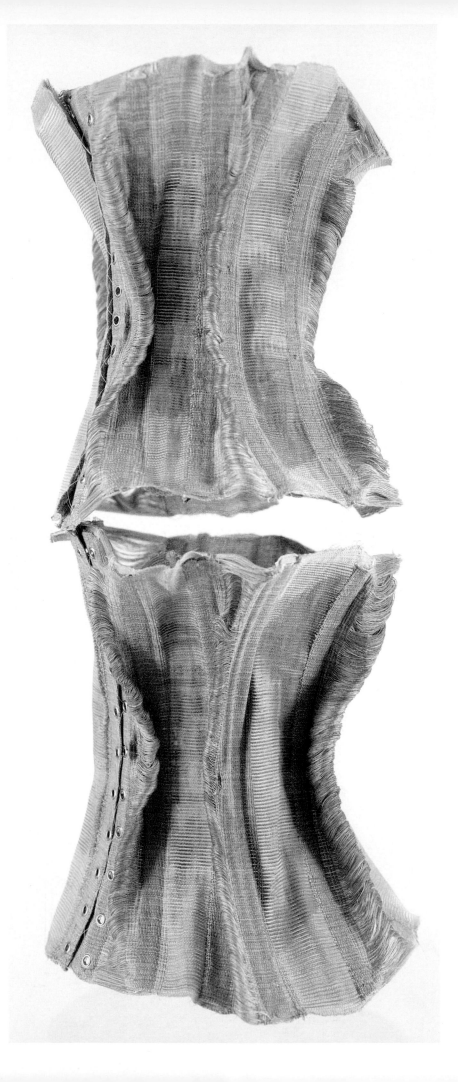

The implications of making and remaking clothes, the handing down and altering of garments are the important qualities in these pieces. They are tensioned into perspex boxes that isolate and preserve the delicate fragmented fabric and which, like the drawers of the conservation museum, protect, conceal and ultimately emphasise a preoccupation with nostalgia and remembering.

Making Clothes for Children 1 was among new work I made for exhibition in Japan at Gallery Gallery in Kyoto. Suddenly the work had become incredibly flat, very fine and almost transparent in its structure. The presentation of these pieces, sandwiched between layers of perspex, serves to emphasise their fine quality, delicate structure and the vulnerability implicit in the choice of materials.

My attention to detail can be painful and I am slightly obsessive in the way that I work, weaving the cloth, working into its surface, unravelling, deconstructing or cutting into the fabric to create the shape that I want. I often weave in layers; triple cloths are a favourite and I often deconstruct them back into separate pieces to emphasise the memories trapped within clothes that we wear, keep or discard.

In this more recent work I not only go back to the dress shape, but also to the garment itself. A fallen hem, a tired and worn seam, a missing button or a lovingly darned and repaired tear are qualities that I am always looking out for. I admire the care that has been taken in repairing, mending and truly recycling fabrics. The resourcefulness of past generations should not be forgotten.

I have often drawn from a small collection of hand-made baby clothes which I found in a junk shop. These garments embody the qualities that I am trying to convey in this later work – vulnerability and the tenderness of making on such a small scale in fragile materials.

Sway Back (1995)
woven, printed and assembled
cotton, polyester and monofilament yarns, polyester boning
35 x 35 x 62cm

***Sway Back* (opposite)
celebrates the relationship
between the medical corset
makers at the Spencer
Corset Factory in Banbury
and their patients. The
underside of the woven
cloth reveals a printed
impression of pelvic x-rays.**

Born   1963, Newcastle-upon-Tyne

Education and Awards

1981-82	Sunderland Polytechnic
1982-85	BA (Hons) Woven and Printed Textiles, West Surrey College of Art and Design, Farnham
1985-86	MA Textiles, Birmingham Polytechnic
1994	Travel award, The British Council in Australia
1998	Research trip to Japan, funded by the British Council and Manchester Metropolitan University, and sponsored by Nippon Airways

Exhibitions: Solo

1994	Showcase exhibition, Canberra School of Art, Australia
1991-3	*A Scrutiny of Constraint,* Derby Art Gallery (tour)

Exhibitions: Group

1998	*Little Revelation*, Gallery Gallery, Kyoto (tour)
1996-8	*Revelation – textile artists addressing issues,* Maidstone Art Gallery, Barbican Art Gallery, London, Museum of Modern Art, Kyoto (tour)
1997	*Knot As They Seam, Permutations in the Fiber Arts*, Maryland Art Place, Baltimore, USA
1996-8	*Art Textiles*, Bury St Edmunds Art Gallery (tour)
1995	*In Our Hands*, Nagoya Trade and Industry Centre, Nagoya
1995	*Unlaced Grace*, Southampton Art Gallery (tour)
1994	*What is Embroidery?*, Whitworth Art Gallery, Manchester
1992-3	*62 Group Retrospective*, Commonwealth Institute, London; Hankyu, Japan (tour)

Professional

1993-	Senior Lecturer, BA (Hons) Contemporary Crafts, Manchester Metropolitan University
1998	Artist-in-Residence and invited speaker, Kawashima Textile School, Kyoto
1994	Textile Artist-in-Residence, Australian National University, Canberra
1990-1	Textile Artist-in-Residence, University of Derby, supported by East Midlands Arts

Work in Collection

Whitworth Art Gallery, University of Manchester
Gallery Gallery, Kyoto

Polly Binns

My work makes allusion to shallow surface, to layerings of water over sand and over mud. My work is an ongoing personal research of the immensity of space and the minutiae of surface. My intention is to pare down the image, to allow contemplation of space.

above:
Tidal Margin (1998) (detail)
linen, painted and stitched
100 x 100cm

left:
Inshore Curve (1996) (detail)
linen, painted and stitched
185 x 125cm

An area of marshland along the north coastline of Norfolk in England forms the main focus for my work. It is a very particular landscape. These marshland flats have been reclaimed by man and are a 'controlled' environment. In order to sustain and stabilise the area 'artificial' elements – sluices, bridges and raised pathways – have been introduced and, by careful negotiation, it is possible to walk, to 'thread' one's way through this isolated space. The quality that particularly draws me to this place is the fact that this marshland is an intertidal zone; twice each day the tide slowly and insidiously fills and 'drowns' the land, irrevocably changing the land surface with its ebb and flow. The seasons of the year also affect the nature of these tides, the pattern of animal and bird life, and the growth and decay of plant life. However much I might wish to re-experience something I have seen, I cannot. The land surface is changed constantly and can never 'be the same'.

This coastline is not my home. I visit throughout the year at regular intervals, sometimes for only a day or two but, when I can, I make visits over consecutive weeks. My practice is to walk repeatedly, tracing and exploring the landscape. I use the pathways and sluices and so on as pointers along my walks, as elements of a repeated experience, places to observe specifics; they act as punctuations along my journey. I try to spend extended periods of time in the landscape. It takes persistence to respond to and reflect on nature's time and scales of movement. The first walk after a gap in time, after a period of urban living and all the other conflicting demands on my life, can be almost a painful experience. So I spend time with a camera, it helps pace my 'seeing' and sharpens my receptiveness. Often it is enough to just look through the lens, without actually taking a photograph.

Another way I focus myself is by working with the land surface itself, changing it, re-arranging it. No record is ever made; I use the activity as a private sketchbook, as a means of consolidating the physical reality of being there – a balance of the observation and the emotional reaction to time and space. Being in the landscape for a long time and by myself is like an 'opening out', a 'lightening'.

I am very aware that part of the sense in my work is to do with this feeling of space. My ambition for the work is that it offers more than a literal, if assimilated, representation of seeing the surface of the sand, the marks of birdlife or the pattern of vegetation. It goes beyond that – it strives to capture a sense of the eternal quality of time and place.

My physical relationship with the landscape is also reflected in the work, within its scale – the memory of my body in the landscape, of my sight line, of my footsteps. This influences the manner in which I work in my studio, the height at which I hang the work as I paint and stitch.

Physical demands are created by working on 'the vertical'. There is a sense of struggle and frustration; process becomes a conscious mark-making, not a soothing or repetitive rhythmic activity. However, the most successful pieces (for me) are those which develop from considerable lengths of time in the 'meditative' process stage, while the actual activity of making happens very rapidly, almost angrily. What goes on to the linen goes straight down, it is not re-worked or changed.

The work is a fusion of my experiences of light, time and passing shadows – those of birds, clouds and boats, a collaboration with shadows. The sense of the grid remains, supporting the rhythm of the stitch marks and being subverted by an increasingly fragmented freedom.

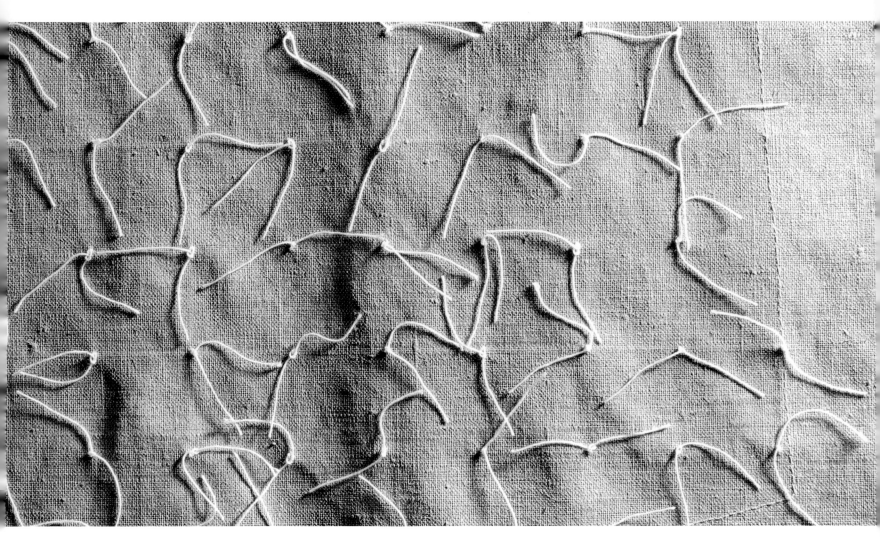

Sand Surface and Shadows Winter 1996 (1996)
(detail)
linen, painted, stitched and split
210 x 280cm

I use the medium and my control over the process to carry my 'image'. These factors are inextricably linked in the intentions for the work, but I also always stay receptive to the inherent potential within the medium released through the process of making. It is this balance, this accrued knowledge, which makes the work essentially 'textile'.

I work with artists' linen, unshrunk, and hung loose upon the studio wall. Because the linen is unshrunk I can exploit its potential for movement when paint is applied, and control its shrinkage process. Hand and machine-based stitches also influence the movement of the surface and the tension of the cloth. There is no prescribed order in which paint or stitch are applied; they are used intuitively according to the individual intentions for a piece. Each process is layered according to the visual tension and image sought. The painting process also affects the visual quality of the stitch applied; the stitching process subverts the degree to which the linen shrinks; both contribute to the whole. Further effects are achieved by working with the linen cloth and thread when wet or dry. The manipulation of the surface involves me working with my fingers, a direct memory of working with and in the landscape.

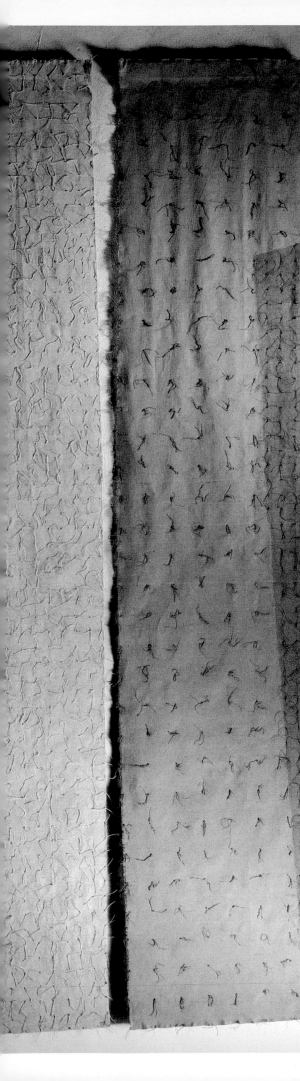

Sand Surface and Shadows Winter 1996 (1996)
linen, painted, stitched and split
210 x 280cm

Sometimes I do take photographs during my walks, responding to whatever chance element is revealed on that particular journey. It might be the way the mud has dried and cracked exposed above a high water mark, lines of debris of marramgrass stranded in curving lines where the tide has receded, patterns of bird footprints, lug-worm holes or even, in the depths of winter, patches of snow left on bridges and pathways. I tend to take photographs in series, responding to one element which dominates on that particular occasion. I keep the photographs in large books in the studio, partly as a reminder, but they are also kept for themselves, as a separate activity. However, they do inevitably form a part of my accumulated memory and I have found that, having completed a piece of work, it possesses qualities about the landscape which I have photographed before and over a protracted period.

I am also aware that as I walk the marsh, 'seeing the landscape', I also 'see' the piece of work to come – it almost intrudes – but I am also conscious that however much I see a piece of work while I am on the marshes, once I am working in the studio the piece will change as it offers its own qualities back to me. Both when I walk and as I work in the studio, there is a sense in which the answers come to me if I let them, if I try to "stop thinking about what I am doing and put my mind to rest". The last line is a quote from the painter Ellsworth Kelly and I very much admire his efforts to articulate this understanding, using the language of words to articulate 'visual language' – an activity outside and beyond words.

Commentary on my work and the manner in which it has been exhibited have engaged it in the debates surrounding 'textile art' and the location of textile art within current visual arts practice. I would say that my work occupies a zone between textiles and fine art which straddles critical thinking around those two areas of practice. It lies, like the tidal foreshore of my inspiration, on an edge, a shifting boundary, interwoven and enriched by both disciplines. Negotiation of my own understanding of my work has tended to be rooted in my visual response to and interest in the work of artists such as Agnes Martin, Mark Rothko, Richard Long and Avis Newman. I draw on it as a way of informing my reading of my own work.

The work which has developed during this past decade out of my intense pre-occupation with and response to this landscape has implicit within it nuances and qualities from earlier work. A first degree in Fine Art, specialising in Sculpture, involved me in explorations around the rigidity and flexibility of materials, and a post-graduate year specialising in ceramics extended this interest. By degrees my work moved into textiles where, during the 1980s, it was characterised by the structural exploration of canvas through paint and stitch. Both media were essentially used as structural influences in the work, as well as performing a decorative role. The ideas were internalized. My current work builds on this understanding and on the skills developed during my earlier years of practice, and should be seen as part of a whole – an extended personal journey.

Sand Sections 1 to 9
**were made between
1995-96. Each section
was created in response
to particular disturbances
of marshland, where
man's activities had
'dug-up' and gouged
the surface.**

The work is not a romantic evocation of my relationship to this marshland coastline but an observation, ongoing personal research of the immensity of space and the minutiae of surface. Creative expression informs my understanding of it and leads the direction of my research. The analysis and control which I exercise over the making process, and its role and importance as a carrier of the image, is fundamental to the work and enriches an understanding of my practice. My fluency lies in my work; my reflections upon the work cannot provide a complete framework, a total understanding. The work leads and has already moved beyond.

Sand Sections No. 8 (1995-96)
linen painted and stitched
from a series of 9, each 29 x 29cm

Born   1950, Kingston-on-Thames, Surrey

Education and Awards

1973-76   BA (Hons) Fine Art, Kingston Polytechnic
1997-98   PhD by completed works, University of Teesside
1984   Artists Travel Award, The British Council
1984   Crafts Council Grant

Exhibitions: Solo

1987   Anatol Orient Gallery, London
1984   *Polly Binns: Fibre Art,* Westminster Gallery, Boston, USA

Exhibitions: Group

1998   *Location,* two-person show with Shirley Chubb, Kings Lynn Arts Centre, Norfolk
1997   *Art of the Stitch,* Barbican Arts Centre, London (tour)
1996   *Visual Relationships*, two-person show with Maggie Henton, Economist Building, London
1996   *Under Construction: Exploring Process in Contemporary Textiles*, Crafts Council, London (tour)
1996   *Take It From Here*, Sunderland City Art Gallery, organised by The Contemporary Art Society
1995   *Out Of This World*, Crafts Council, London (tour)
1994   *Inscape*, two-person show, Midlands Arts Centre, Birmingham (tour)
1992   *Out Of The Frame*, Crafts Council, London (tour)
1992   *62 Group: New Textile Art,* Commonwealth Institute, London (tour)
1990   *62 Group*, Collins Gallery, University of Strathclyde, Glasgow
1989   *The Art of Embroidery*, University of Wales, Aberystwyth
1986   *Fibre Art*, Central Museum of Textiles, Lodz, Poland
1985   *Internationale Kunsthandwerk,* Internationale Kunstmesse, Bergdorf, Switzerland
1983   *British Needlework*, National Museum of Modern Art, Kyoto
1982   *Stitchery*, British Crafts Centre, London

Commissions

1993   22 works located in San Francisco, Seaport, N.Y. and Michigan, commissioned by Liz Claiborne Inc, USA
1989   Textile hanging for Head Office, ICI
1989   Four-funnelled form, commissioned by Trafalgar House plc

Professional

1993-   Senior Lecturer, Faculty of Design, Chilterns University College, Buckinghamshire
1992-97   Member of Council, Crafts Council

Work in Collection

                    Museum of Modern Art, Kyoto
                    Crafts Council, London
                    Whitworth Art Gallery, University of Manchester

Sally Freshwater

Much of the preparation work for these projects is reliant on computer 'drawing' and all the hidden information which this involves. Understanding the materials allows for a fluency in the language. I have found parallels in the thinking of some contemporary architects, sympathetic ways of dealing with space, and a purity and acknowledgement of materials and their inherent values.

Installation for Atrium (1996)
commissioned for Burmah Castrol Headquarters, Swindon
cotton sailcloth, embroidered detail, aluminium
in collaboration with Architen

Working with pliable materials to create objects and shapes with volume and form has always been the main driving force behind my work. A solid training in textiles provided the skills base from which my current working practice has evolved, although I recognised early on that I was exploring an area largely outside the conventions of the majority of textile courses. While the basic technical processes were the same the motivation was focused elsewhere: I needed pattern-cutting but not in relation to garments; stitch was very important in understanding the relationship between the thread and the cloth, but it was functional rather than decorative; structure was important and potentially encompassed many of the resources of the Fine Art workshop.

I was also very conscious of artists working with pliable materials, such as Eva Hesse, Robert Morris and Richard Smith. Exciting things were happening in Poland involving vast tapestries, and the perception there of this kind of work was different; it was recognised as being something other than design, closer to painting and sculpture. And there were aspects of architecture, particularly the structures of Frei Otto, which held some of the values I wanted to explore.

I began by looking at the functional nature of certain materials themselves and the various skills that have evolved for their handling and manipulation for particular usage. I discovered that the degree of knowledge possessed by some experts could only be learned by handling and working the fabrics in order to understand their intrinsic qualities. The sail-maker, for example, knew how much slack to allow in the seam of the cloth to permit the sail to work effectively with the wind. Through repeated handling of the raw materials over many years of learning his craft the kite-maker understood what combination of bamboo, paper and thread would create a kite that could master the wind. The very specific combination of structural elements and tensioned fabric in tents began to give me the clues to the language I required.

The scope for the use of textiles in architecture extended as new fabrics were developed, and this seemed to happen at the same time as the scale of possibilities developed for my own work. The evolution of digital modelling and new technically advanced fabrics have allowed the architect to develop highly realistic and technically precise models. Computer drawing can generate the shape of a structure, analyse its behaviour under changing load condition and produce a detailed geometry of each component, providing the cutting patterns for the fabrics.

Uses of fabric which began as hand-crafted, knowledge-based skills have advanced at a tremendous pace with the assistance of computers and this evolution has been important to the realisation of my larger site-specific works. Much of the preparation work for these projects is reliant on computer 'drawing' and all the hidden information which this involves.

Understanding the materials allows for a fluency in the language. The pieces I make are deceptively simple but exploit the inherent qualities of the materials used. All the elements are interdependent. The precision of the stitch, perfection of the fabric surface and accuracy of the construction is vital, allowing the form and the atmosphere of the work to dominate.

My interest and excitement with the large scale is partly to do with the cooperative nature of such projects, the physicality of handling the materials, and the need for the involvement of expertise from other areas. Large works are never fully resolved until all the elements come together, and this often takes place during the installation itself, so they require a degree of faith and courage throughout the making process.

Mobile (1996)
commissioned by Highgate Group Practice
aluminium, ripstop nylon
three spirals,150, 175, 200cm high
each 100cm diameter

My current body of work explores the intrinsic qualities of a material and what it can do, manipulates the stresses and strains, the warp and weft, and looks at how these pieces relate to the body through a particular scale, the way in which they occupy your field of vision. I have found parallels in the thinking of some contemporary architects, sympathetic ways of dealing with space, and a purity and acknowledgement of materials and their inherent values.

My ideas evolve through drawing, often a shorthand form of linear sketches, sometimes measured diagrams on graph paper, model-making and manipulation of materials, which requires practical experience of the fabrics to know how a surface feels and will behave, and how one material works visually with another. Long periods away from the studio are very disquieting. I need to be making, working very directly with the fabrics. This is usually where the germ of an idea starts.

above:
Hush (1994)
toughspun, aluminium
200 x 100 x 27cm

The pieces I make are deceptively simple but exploit the inherent qualities of the materials used. All the elements are interdependent. The precision of the stitch, perfection of the fabric surface and accuracy of the construction is vital, allowing the form and the atmosphere of the work to dominate.

My work seems to be divided into work created for exhibition and that made for site-specific commission. But while the form of the outcome may appear different, the underlying concerns are always the same. Paramount to any piece is space and scale. If the site for a work is non-specific then the relationship of the viewer to the work becomes more important: whether the work is small and intimate or very large, dominating the field of vision. The spatial relationships are extremely important. Each piece is about scale: the scale of the work, the scale in relation to the viewer and, by implication, to me as the artist. The intention is to provide a focus. They are deliberately abstract, not replicating other forms, although the shapes and materials may echo familiar objects, creating associations in the mind of the viewer. Many works have an implied movement, which has become a real element in some pieces.

The commission for the Highgate Group Practice provided the opportunity to work with forms that would be in constant motion. Spatially, it also offered the challenge of a work that is visible from a number of vantage points, so I worked with the idea of creating forms that were very different depending on the point from which they are seen; the final mobile assumes one shape as you walk into the surgery, but appears quite different from the floor of the waiting room below it. The colour in this work is also important to the environment for which it was created, and this and the shapes were developed partly in response to a painting owned by the practice.

Rock is a very different piece using movement. It was commissioned for an exhibition at the Oriel Gallery in Cardiff and, partly due to its scale, has not been shown since. At over nine metres long, it has a very calming rhythmic movement, responding to oscillating air-currents from a remote fan. The form and the materials are very simple and pure, with many echoes. This is probably my favourite work.

below:
C. Scape (1998)
formed lead
75 x 75cm

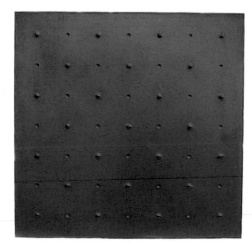

Work made for exhibition fulfils very different criteria from commissioned pieces; it is on the whole more self-centred, providing the opportunity to explore and experiment with ideas and forms, and may perhaps exist only for one or two shows, so the materials can be less permanent and the structures less robust. Site-specific commissions, however, have to be developed in discussion with the client and there are considerations in relation to the site that cannot be ignored. For public spaces, some materials are not acceptable, and I have to think about maintenance, the function of the space and the complications of installation etc as I begin to develop ideas. In many ways it is not so different to working for an exhibition but I have a different set of ground rules to start from.

"We are enveloped by the gigantic, surrounded by it, enclosed within its shadow. Whereas we know the miniature as a spatial whole, we know the gigantic only partially."
(Susan Stewart, *On Longing*)

My interest and excitement with the large scale is also about the cooperative nature of such projects, the physicality of handling the materials and the need for the involvement of expertise from areas other than art to realise an idea. Large works are never fully resolved until all the elements come together, and this often takes place during the installation itself, so they require a degree of faith and courage throughout the making process.

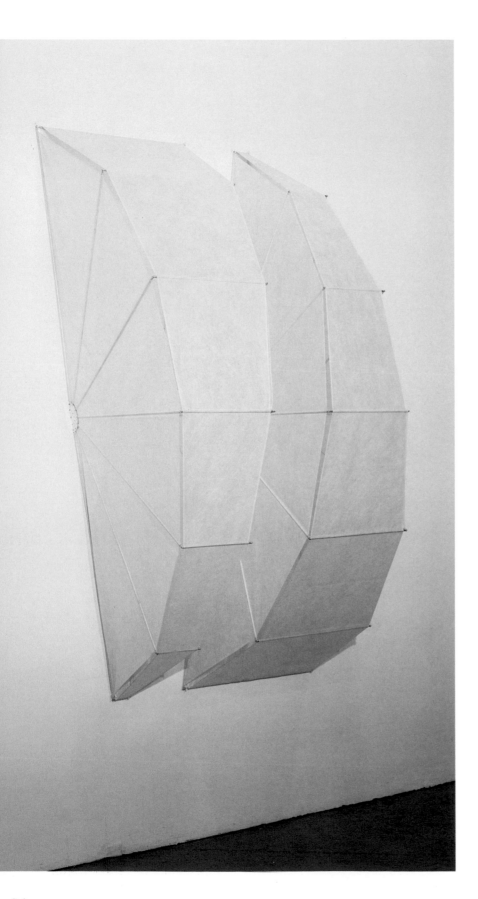

It is important to work with people whom I trust and who understand what I am trying to do through the work, as some of these projects involve many people and much creative time. Misunderstandings can be disappointing and costly.

As the scale of my work has increased through commissions it has forced me to relinquish much of the making to other people – architects, structural engineers, sail-makers, riggers and even mountaineers – in order to realise a site-specific work. For these projects the bulk of my creative work happens in the early stages, through drawings, prototype sections, sampling and model making, and in discussion with the client and the team that will ultimately make and install the final work.

While I take great care in ensuring the materials I use will withstand the demands of the location in which the works are placed, it is disappointing when they are not maintained. Though I may relinquish ownership of the works once they are completed, they are nevertheless in the public gaze and their appearance is very important to me. The way in which they are maintained is a reflection of the owner's commitment to the artist and, sometimes, this slips out of the picture.

Studio time often feels like a luxury and a self-indulgence, particularly if there is no specific outcome from a body of work. Sometimes the balance shifts and other activities become more dominant but, ultimately, I am a maker and it is only this manual activity that satisfies a very basic drive. As Anish Kapoor has said, "it is about looking for an internal language, a relationship between what one does and what one feels."

I am still working on that relationship.

White Kin (1996)
toughspun, aluminium
200 x 100 x 25cm

Born   1958, Bedford, Bedfordshire

Education and Awards

1975-77	Mander College, Bedford
1977-80	BA (Hons) Goldsmiths College, University of London
1980-82	MA Royal College of Art, London
1985	Crafts Council Setting-up Grant

Exhibitions: Solo

1994	*Margins*, The Economist Building, London

Exhibitions: Group

1998	*Cloths of Gold,* Contemporary Applied Arts, London
1997	Co-curator of *Contemporary Artists Showcase 2 Exhibition*, Riverside Studios
1996	*Beyond the Bounds*, Manchester Metropolitan University and Maidstone Art Gallery
1996	Two-person exhibition with Julie Wood at Contemporary Applied Arts, London
1996	*Under Construction*, Crafts Council Gallery, London (tour)
1996	*Sally Freshwater: Julie Wood,* Oriel Gallery, Cardiff
1995	*Working with Paper,* Bury St.Edmunds Art Gallery (tour)

Commissions

Gatwick Airport, Arrivals Concourse, South Terminal
W.H. Smith Distribution Centre, Swindon, Reception Dome
Bradford and Bingley Head Office in Bingley, West Yorkshire, Atrium Sculpture
Exchange House in Broadgate, sculpture for two atria
Tabor School, Braintree, Essex, two sculptures with Rushton Aust
Atrium commission for Burmah Castrol, Swindon
Atrium commission for the Highgate Group Practice, London

Work in Collection

BAA
Burmah Castrol
Crafts Council of Great Britain
W.H. Smith
Embroiderers' Guild, London
Rosehaugh Stanhope Developments
Bradford and Bingley
Whitworth Art Gallery, Manchester

Professional

Senior Lecturer, Applied and Media Arts, University of Hertfordshire
Visiting Lecturer, Textile Art, Winchester School of Art

Alice Kettle

**My work is a search for balance, for rhythmic harmony, a desire for lyrical movement, and a quest for beauty borrowed from light and colour.
It is an optimistic stance.**

above:
Basking Aphrodite (1993)
stitched cotton, silk, rayon, metallic thread
33 x 44cm

left:
In Camera (1996-7)
Scottish High Court, Lawnmarket, Edinburgh
four folded stitched wall-hangings
maximum dimensions 450cm x 10m

My work is simply an observation of where I stand at any moment. It is a purely personal comment on the human condition. Sometimes my work is about vulnerability; at other times, about a contained poise and strength, or the exuberance of movement. Through my sewing machine I can express all my perceptions of the world. Any hard-won fluency I have gained in the machine's own magical vocabulary gives me the courage to say what I cannot say in words.

My work has until recently been entirely peopled with figures. They can be an impressionistic response to an experience of a place: an attempt to capture the paradoxes of India, where the richness of intense and heightened colour vies for attention with the stark, ubiquitous poverty; or, the vastness of the Australian ochre landscape and the brightness of the sunlight. Some earlier pieces were about me, not in a representational sense, but simply to explore who I am.

What unites my work is a desire to understand my own motivations, and those of others. My work is a search for balance, for rhythmic harmony, a desire for lyrical movement, and a quest for beauty borrowed from light and colour. It is an optimistic stance. I view the creative act as something awesome and miraculous. It carries with it aspirations for a kind of timeless balance and an acknowledgment of the environment around us.

My stance has shifted: whereas I used to be a painter, now I am an artist who uses stitch. I used to paint huge canvases, layering the paint and using very strong colour. As a painter I was encouraged to work on a large scale, and understood the potency of a drawn line. Now this sense of potency has simply been transferred from my brush to the needle of my sewing machine: I draw with the needle and fabric as though I am moving the paper under the pen.

A sewing machine has two sources of thread, top and bottom. By continually changing the tensions between them and by blending cotton, metallic, silk threads, the surface texture can be changed and colours blended with subtlety. Changes in thread tension give a sense of fluid movement which is a characteristic of the textile surface. As parts of the surface stand out in three-dimensional relief, plays of light and shadow emerge once the work is hung. Sometimes I extend this three-dimensional effect further by folding the hangings away from the wall, as in In Camera (opposite and p 86), where a wooden substructure is behind the hangings, thus they curve away from the wall in a variety of shapes. It gives the impression of ambiguity – solid or fluid?

I find the rhythmic process of machine stitching suits my psyche, the long periods of stitching become a reflective, almost meditative, creative time. I can build a person out of a mass of thread and create his environment. I can allow the rhythms of stitch to form gradually with the folds in the fabric. When I feel impatient I just use some thick thread. There have certainly been changes in my style over the past few years – with an ongoing search to break away from a flat surface. I have attempted to recapture the directness of paint with the added qualities offered by the substance and the surface of thread.

In Camera (page 86) was commissioned by the Scottish Court Service for the High Court in Edinburgh. The brief was for a large work which would hold the interest of the casual visitor as well as of those working there every day.

The left-hand panel represents the group of 15 jurors. The next panel is the Judge, while the right hand panel is visitors to the court. Each hanging is folded or curved away from the wall on a wooden substructure, to give a shifting viewpoint.

I was captivated by the theatricality of the court. Each figure is seen from the waist up, a splash of colour on a soft curving background. The blue draws the sky down into the building, bringing in the outside world. I wanted to convey a sense of hope in the face of justice.

In Camera (1996-7) (detail of a Juror)
Scottish High Court, Lawnmarket, Edinburgh
four folded stitched wall-hangings
maximum dimensions 450cm x 10m

Previously the figure was the defining part of the work, and the flow of the background followed the line of the figure. The balance and attitude of the limbs were the focus. Recently I have started with the background, and only then do I start introducing the figure. The face is often lost over the edge of the piece, and the limbs connect with the landscape or background. The implication is that we are defined by our situation and circumstance.

I feel myself to be a contemporary artist, that is both working with modern materials and aware of the social dilemmas around us. After all, thirty years ago I would not have been able to work as I do. I would have had to couch metal threads on to the surface. I would not have been able to stitch the metallic threads through the fabric using a sewing machine, mixing them with cottons, rayons, silks, seducing the play of light on this pliant surface.

I am conscious of a tension between the desires and potentials created by new technologies, with the sometimes conflicting consciousness of the environment and of spiritual values. I wish to attain balance. I am dependent on a machine, and at the same time I aspire to fluidity of self-expression. I feel as though my machine and I have reached a kind of understanding. It always used to be like taming a horse, breaking the unruly will of this animal, to become its master.

Born   1961, Winchester, Hampshire

Education and Awards

1979-84	BA (Hons) Fine Art, University of Reading
1985-86	Postgraduate Diploma in Textile Art, Goldsmiths College, University of London
1987-97	Southern Arts (five awards)
1991	British Council Grant
1999	Winner of Bernina Award
1999	Winner of Kreinik Award

Exhibitions

1999	*Art of the Stitch*, Barbican Art Gallery, London (tour)
1998	*Knot As They Seam*, *Permutations in the Fiber Arts*, Maryland Art Place, Baltimore, USA
1998	*Stitch*, Bury St Edmunds Art Gallery
1998	Two person show with Carol Naylor, Otter Gallery, West Sussex Institute, Chichester
1998	*UK Now*, Melbourne, Australia
1997	*Art of the Stitch*, Barbican Art Gallery, London (tour)
1996	*William Morris Revisited,* Whitworth Art Gallery, Manchester, Crafts Council, London (tour)

Commissions

1999-2000	*Tree of Knowledge*, National Library of Australia, Canberra
1999-2000	Three altar frontals for the High Altar, Gloucester Cathedral
1995-7	*In Camera*, High Court, Lawnmarket, Edinburgh
1994	Altar frontal for the Holy Sepulchre Chapel, Winchester Cathedral
1994-5	*Glimpses of India*, m.v. Oriana, P&O Cruises

Professional

1997	Artist-in-Residence, Canberra School of Art, Australia
1987-	Visiting Lecturer, Goldsmiths College; Royal College of Art, London; Winchester School of Art

Work in Collection

Whitworth Art Gallery, Manchester
Crafts Council of Great Britain
Embroiderers' Guild, London
St Mary's College, Baltimore, USA
Somerville College, Oxford University

Publications

1997	Ilze Aviks, 'The Embroidery Art of Alice Kettle', *FIBERARTS* (N. Carolina, USA)
1995	Jennifer Harris, *Eye of the Needle, the Textile Art of Alice Kettle* (Telos, Winchester)
1993	Jennifer Harris (ed.), *5000 Years of Textiles* (London, British Museum Press)
1992	Chloë Colchester, *The New Textiles* (London, Thames and Hudson)

opposite:
Man & Tree I (1998) (detail)
stitched cotton, metallic &
rayon thread onto cotton canvas
320 x 225cm

Other specialist textile publications from Telos Art Publishing

ART TEXTILES OF THE WORLD

Art Textiles of the World: USA
Edited by Matthew Koumis, Essay by Ilze Aviks
Kyoung Ae Cho, Virginia Davis, Deborah Fisher, Ann Hamilton, Linda Hutchins,
Charlene Nemec-Kessel, Jane Lackey, Susan Lordi Marker, Jason Pollen, Jane Sauer
ISBN 0 9526267 1 3   286 x 242mm, 108pp, 50 col. illus. softback   £25   (2000)

Art Textiles of the World: Australia
Edited by Matthew Koumis, Essay by Professor Sue Rowley
Utopia Awely Batik Aboriginal Corporation, Patricia Black, Elena Gallegos, Pam Gaunt,
Ruth Hadlow, Jan Irvine Nealie, Elsje King, Valerie Kirk, Tori de Mestre, Patrick Snelling
ISBN 0 9526267 0 5   286 x 242mm, 108pp, 52 col. illus. softback £25   (1999)

Art Textiles of the World: Japan
Edited by Matthew Koumis, Essay by Keiko Kawashima
Masae Bamba, Machiko Agano, Yasuko Fujino, Masashi Honda, Haruko Honma, Masakazu
and Naomi Kobayashi, Kiyonori Shimada, Hiroyuki Shindo, Yuko Takada, Chiyoko Tanaka,
Mitsuo Toyazaki, Chiyu Uemae
ISBN 0 9526267 4 8   286 x 242mm, 128pp, 118 col. illus. softback   £25   (1997)

Art Textiles of the World: Great Britain Volume One
Edited by Matthew Koumis, Essay by Amanda Fielding
Jeanette Appleton, Jo Barker, Kate Blee, Sara Brennan, Dawn Dupree, Sally Greaves-Lord,
Nicola Henley, Greg Parsons, Marta Rogoyska, Lynn Setterington
ISBN 0 9526267 2 1   286 x 242mm, 112pp, 100 col. illus. softback   (1996)

In preparation:

Art Textiles of the World: Holland (2001)
Edited by Dery Timmer

Art Textiles of the World: Scandinavia (2002)
Edited by Matthew Koumis

Art Textiles of the World: India (2004)
Edited by Nita Thakore

Comments about other titles from Telos

Your publications are brilliant. I was in Australia for the opening of the show based on your Australian book. The exhibit was beautiful and the book extraordinary. I am an enthusiastic supporter of the contribution you are making to the field of art textiles. If there is no recorded history, the work is quickly forgotten.
Jane Sauer, Textile Artist and Curator, USA

This is not just a coffee table book. It is a reference book, an inspiration and a good read.
Judith Butt, World of Embroidery, England

Thank you so much for the book, it is a splendid volume and beautifully produced, we have included it in our library.
Eulalia Morral, Director, Museo Textil, Terrassa, Spain

We can be grateful to Koumis for putting strong images into circulation. He clearly works from a sense of passion and commitment.
Pamela Johnson, Crafts, England

Another superb title in this impressive series...hugely varied and evocative art works. Telos is such a classy publisher.
Janet De Boer, Textile Fibre Forum, Australia

A beautiful and sophisticated book, very inspiring!
Jo Barker, Tapestry Weaver, Scotland

Thank you for the beautifully published catalogue Take 4 on British quilt art.
Hanny Spierenburg, TextielPlus, Holland

This is a truly wonderful book. The rich vibrancy of the aboriginal batik is stunning...a beautiful book for serious lovers of textile art.
Sue Thompson, Needlecraft, England

Thank you very much – I've never seen such a beautiful book about Japanese fiber art before – all very artistic. Your book itself is an art.
Koichi Kawashima, Teacher and Artist, Japan

People responded to the book with utter delight and it was surprisingly apt as an accompaniment to the show.
Hannah Bilton, ArtSway, England

What a beautiful book on Japan!
Kristen Dibbs, Textile Artist and Author, Australia

This beautiful book....
Country Living

Thank you so much for the wonderful book on Japanese textiles. It is excellent and has been much admired at our last textile symposium meeting.
Valerie Kirk, Tapestry Weaver and Head of Textiles, Australian National University, Canberra

Many thanks for the prompt despatch of Art Textiles of the World: Australia. It is an inspiring volume, and already read from cover to cover lifted my spirits. I start my week with a light heart and creative determination.
Olga Norris, Artist, England